PERSONAL SUCCESS

The Promise of God

Victor Matthews

ISBN: 0-8010-6247-0

Formerly published under the title:
Growth in Grace

Preface

Personal success is the promise of God! "And ye shall know the truth, and the truth shall make you free" (John 8:32).

Christians have the liberty, the ability, the right to become the kind of persons that God had in mind when He created us. Instead of being enslaved by our sin, crippled by our ignorance, and bound by our tensions, we may enjoy the freedom God has promised.

The truth shall make you free! God has revealed the truth to us through the person of His Son Jesus Christ and it is recorded in the Bible. There is no need to stumble, grope, and guess about the truth.

To know the truth will make us free. Knowledge, truth, freedom—these head the list of any system of values. And that is the reason for this book. You can know the truth and you can have the freedom of personal success. If you will honestly study the Bible and consistently apply it to your daily life, God will transform you as a person. The material you hold in your hand has been carefully prepared to lead you step by step into the knowledge of the truth which will make you free!

Contents

Chapter 1

The Nature of Biblical Christianity

A *disturbing question:* Do I know the meaning of biblical Christianity?

It is very possible for an earnest Christian to be so poorly taught and so confused about the truths of Christianity that he is unable to adequately practice the Christian life.

One of the major sources of weakness, disappointment, and frustration in the life of the Christian stems from failure to understand the nature of biblical Christianity. What we do not know we cannot practice or enjoy. True worship is governed by truth, and the truth must be learned.

Those who work with the laws of physics must know their field. They must learn the nature and characteristics of the laws which pertain to their area of specialization. It is not sufficient to guess. There is no substitute for knowledge in the life of the engineer, the physicist, the mathematician, or the physician. Nor is it enough for the young man to have a desire to build a bridge. He must learn the laws which govern bridge building and how to put these laws into practice.

The Christian, likewise, must have more than a desire to live successfully. The desire, no matter how great, is not enough. As the engineer, he must learn the truths of Christianity and how to put them into practice. Only then will he have the conditions which will enable him to live successfully.

One important factor which has led to a misunderstanding of Christianity is the failure to distinguish between biblical principle and "Christian" practice. What Christians and churches practice is not necessarily the truth. One must learn to evaluate the statements and beliefs of Christians and churches by the principles and truths of the Bible. Many Christians and non-Christians have been confused by poor teaching and poor practice.

It is well to ask the question, "Do I know the meaning of biblical Christianity?" There are many who are not willing to ask such a question and there are many more who cannot give an adequate answer.

Any hesitancy in this area can lead only to failure.

A basic assumption: Christianity is based on divine revelation.

Christianity has not been given to us as a lump of clay which may be molded into innumerable

8

shapes. God has revealed Himself to us in and through Jesus Christ. This revelation forms the foundation, the structure, and the content of genuine Christianity. It comes to us as final authority.

Since genuine Christianity is the result of an authoritative revelation, it is evident that any tampering with or faulty interpretation of its basic message can result only in the production of a false Christianity. It is obvious, as one looks about the religious world today, that this is exactly what has happened.

The importance of this assumption can hardly be overemphasized. The authority for belief and practice is divine revelation. This authority, therefore, does not reside in the church, nor in the leaders of the church, nor in religious experience, whether it be personal or corporate. God is truth and He has made Himself and His will known. This revelation has been authoritatively recorded in the Scriptures.

To be a genuine Christian and to live a successful Christian life, we must begin, as an engineer, with the acceptance of a final authority. We must bow in complete submission before God and His revelation. No engineer may select the laws which meet his approval and reject the rest. To be successful he must accept all the laws and their authoritative demands. And so it is with the Christian.

Untold damage has resulted due to the negligence of engineers, physicians, and men in similar professions. Far greater damage is to be found in the spiritual realm. Men and women have based their lives and destinies on false interpretations of

9

the Bible. Life, talent, time, and money have been wasted. Freedom, power, and progress follow the knowledge and practice of the truth. When truth is not known and ignorance is practiced, only harm can follow.

God has made Himself known to us in Jesus Christ through history as recorded in Scripture. This is where we must start. We must be willing to go to this final authority and to test our belief and practice. (See Diagram 1.)

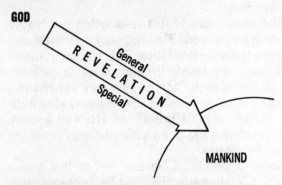

GOD

REVELATION
General
Special

MANKIND

Diagram 1. God has revealed Himself in two ways: general and special revelation. By general revelation we mean those evidences within the creation such as design, stability of law, human values, and conscience which point to the Creator (Ps. 19:1; Rom. 1:20; 2:14, 15). God has revealed Himself in His work.

By special revelation we refer to the many communications of divine truth whereby God has revealed Himself as the Redeemer of His people. This process of special revelation culminated in the incarnation of Jesus Christ as the living Word, and in the completion of the written Word, the Bible, (I Cor. 15:1-4; Heb. 1:1-3). Unless otherwise stated, the term *revelation* is used in this book to indicate special revelation.

The key to success: accept and obey the revelation of God as final authority.

10

An important perspective: Christianity revolves around a person, Jesus Christ.

In the Old Testament days it was the pre-incarnate Christ who said to Abraham, "... *I* am thy shield and thy exceeding great reward" (Gen. 15:1). He said to Moses, "... Certainly *I* will be with thee ..." (Exod. 3:12). He spoke to Israel by Hosea and said, "... in *me* is thine help" (Hos. 13:9). Through Jeremiah He spoke to Judah and said, "... they have forsaken *me* the fountain of living water ..." (Jer. 2:13, italics mine).

The message of the New Testament is the same. The Lord Jesus Christ said to Peter and Andrew, "... Follow *me* ..." (Matt. 4:19). He said, "Come unto *me* ... and *I* will give you rest" (Matt. 11:28). He also said, "... *I* am the light of the world ..." (John 8:12); "... *I* am the resurrection, and the life ..." (John 11:25); "... *I* am the way, the truth, and the life ..." (John 14:6); "... without *me* ye can do nothing" (John 15:5, italics mine).

The same emphasis is found in the apostolic interpretation of Christianity. John said, "But as many as received *him*, to them gave *he* power to become the sons of God, even to them that believe *on his name*" (John 1:12). It was Peter who said, "According as his divine power hath given unto us all things that pertain unto life and godliness, through the knowledge of *him* ..." (II Peter 1:3). Paul taught that God has blessed us with all spiritual blessings "... *in Christ*" (Eph. 1:3), and he prayed that the Christians might be illuminated and grow, "... in the knowledge *of Him*" (Eph. 1:17). Of his own spiritual life Paul said,

11

". . . *Christ* liveth in me . . ." (Gal. 2:20); "For to me to live is *Christ* . . ." (Phil. 1:21); and "That I may know *him* . . ." (Phil. 3:10, italics mine).

The identical message is proclaimed in the doctrinal explanation of Christianity. Jesus Christ is the object of faith (Acts 16:31); the source of all wisdom and knowledge (Col. 2:3); the Savior of mankind (I John 4:14); the Head of the church (Eph. 1:22); the believer's peace (Eph. 2:14); his wisdom, righteousness, sanctification, and redemption (I Cor. 1:30); his power (I Cor. 1:24); and the One in whom all believers are complete (Col. 2:10).

Christianity is surely a belief, a group of doctrines, a relationship, an ethic, a way of life, a form of service, a living hope, a demanding imperative, and a transforming deliverance, but all of these are rooted in and revolve around the person of Jesus Christ, the Son of God. Christianity is first of all Jesus Christ (see Diagram 2).

A serious warning: Christianity is often perverted.

Religious perversions are not produced by agnostics or atheists but by well-meaning Christians. In the attempt to cure some failure in practice, one facet of biblical Christianity has often been overemphasized. When this facet is made the central factor in Christianity, a perversion results. There are at least four common perversions taught in the church today.

(1) One of the most common perversions is the misconception that Christianity revolves around

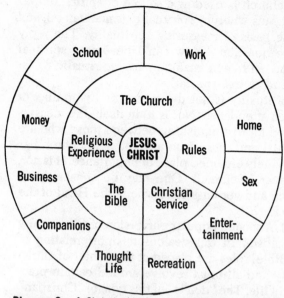

Diagram 2. A Christian's life is centered in the person of Jesus Christ. All areas of life must revolve around Him.

The key to success: accept and obey the will of God. Jesus Christ is to have preeminence in all things (Col. 1:18).

the church. Even a casual reading of the New Testament will indicate the importance of this divine institution. God, however, did not bring the church into existence to be at the center of our lives. That place must be reserved for and filled by Jesus Christ, the Head of the church. There are many today who have given the place of Christ to the church. In misplaced zeal they have taken that which is secondary and made it first.

When the church is made the central factor in Christianity, it is utilized in at least three ways.

13

The church is used as a source of spirituality, as the means whereby spirituality is maintained, and as the basis of measuring spirituality. The reply to the question, "How can I become a spiritual person and then maintain my spirituality?" is: "Attend church regularly."

Spirituality is not the automatic by-product of church attendance. Nor is it, in itself, the measuring rod for distinguishing between those who are spiritual and those who are not. The church has its divinely ordained place of importance. It is not, however, a cure-all. One may be constantly in church and yet miss Him who is the Head of the church.

(2) A second popular perversion of Christianity is legalism. In this zealous misinterpretation of the Bible, rules are placed at the center of Christianity and all must revolve around certain practices of life. The "don'ts" of this type of "Christian" life receive undue emphasis. The Christian is one who has stopped doing certain things!

The key to spirituality, for this way of thinking, is the wholehearted acceptance of certain rules as absolutes. Obedience to these rules is a guarantee as well as the mark of spirituality.

There is no question about the emphasis of the Bible on obedience. And there are many commandments in Scripture which the Christian must obey. However, these commandments are not an end in themselves. They have been given to us as the means whereby we obey God. The Christian is not to obey the commandment alone. He is to obey God—by keeping the commandment. This is the reason why love and obedience are inseparably related in the Bible (John 14:15, 21, 23; 15:10; I John 2:5; 5:3; II John 6).

The legalist is almost never content to stop with the commandments of Scripture. New rules must be invented which are somehow twisted into becoming the application of biblical principles. God, love, and personal freedom are soon eclipsed. It is frightfully easy to obey all the rules of the legalist and even the commandments of the Bible and yet not give first place to one's Lord.

(3) A third perversion of Christianity may be called emotionalism or the overemphasis on religious experience. A certain type of experience may be proclaimed as the secret of spirituality and as the distinguishing mark of spiritual people. In this way a personal subjective authority is substituted for the authority of divine revelation. To have an inner feeling of spirituality and to be able to produce at will some manifestation of religious zeal may be a great comfort to some people but it is not described in the Bible as being of the essence of Christianity.

Religious experiences and emotional feelings are surely a part of biblical Christianity. These, however, are the *results* and not the causes of the work of grace. A person is not necessarily right with God simply because his emotion so testifies. Non-Christians have been known to produce elaborate and sustained religious experiences.

When Christianity is made to revolve around emotionalism or religious experience, and not around the person of Jesus Christ, there is the ever-present danger of shifting the standard of authority from God and His revelation to ourselves and our experiences. One may be so preoccupied with his experience that he may bypass Christ, the believer's sanctification (I Cor. 1:30).

(4) A fourth illustration of how Christianity may suffer from perversion is the overemphasis on Christian service. A certain type or types of service may be placed at the center of Christianity. Here Christian service becomes the source of spirituality and the manner whereby it is maintained. The spiritual people are those who perform a stereotyped service which usually revolves around the church.

There is no question but that Scripture pronounces a commission over every Christian. To be a Christian is to be a worker. However, what was said above about obeying God may also be said here. Christian service is not an end in itself. This is only one way whereby God is loved, worshiped, and obeyed—in practice. It is all too easy to be intensely engaged in service and yet not be serving God. Many times it is the church which is being served, or the pastor, or even our own conscience.

Christianity does not revolve around a form of service; it revolves around the person of Jesus Christ. It is possible to be taken up with a great variety of Christian services and yet not be committed to the Lord of the harvest field.

As Christians we must take a very firm stand against ourselves and against the perversions of Christianity. It is sinfully easy to transfer our love and devotion from God to something associated with God. When this happens we are more in love with religion than with God! Only He may be the object of our affection. (See Diagram 3.)

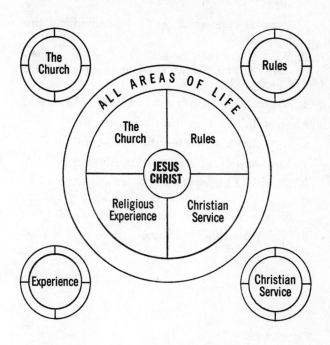

Diagram 3. The church may not be at the center of life because Jesus Christ is the Head of the church (Eph. 1:22).

Rules may not be at the center of life because Jesus Christ is our Lord (Luke 6:46).

Religious experience may not be at the center of life because Jesus Christ is our sanctification (I Cor. 1:30).

Christian service may not be at the center of life because Jesus Christ is the Lord of the harvest field (Matt. 9:38).

The key to success: give Jesus Christ His rightful place (Rom. 12:1, 2).

Questions for Discussion

1. What is the basic essential for living the Christian life?

2. What is the great bedrock underlying true Christianity?

3. What is the rule for belief and practice in the Christian life? Can we mold Christianity to fit our culture and situations?

4. Where do we begin to test our beliefs and practices?

5. What did Jesus say that Christianity is?

6. How does a person become a child of God?

7. How do we maintain our spirituality?

8. Should we be legalists? Why, or why not?

9. What place should religious feelings and emotional experiences hold in the Christian life?

10. What place should Christian service hold in a believer's life?

Chapter 2

The Nature of Biblical Christianity

The biblical description: Christianity is final authority.

Christianity is not an institution, not a list of rules, not a religious experience, and not a certain type of service. Christianity revolves around a person, Jesus Christ, the Son of God.

When one asks, "What does this mean in practice?" the biblical answer is "final authority."

The engineer and the physicist are inescapably and rigidly limited by the laws of nature. They will succeed only by carefully working in harmony with these laws. They are under an authority which is external to them and over which they have no control. The engineer may have an intense dislike for concrete. But this personal dislike does not give him license to build a bridge out of papier mâché.

And so it is in Christianity. God has revealed Himself. This revelation is no less authoritative than the laws of physics. It is, in fact, much more so. Scripture is emphatically clear on the necessity of repentance, the new birth, faith, love, confession of sin, and obedience. In these areas the right and the wrong has been clearly stated. The Christian may not live as though God has not spoken, as though Jesus Christ has not come, as though the crucifixion and the resurrection did not happen, as though the Bible were not written.

It would be ridiculous for the airplane builder to think that he could operate successfully without taking into account the laws of gravity. It would be even more ridiculous for the Christian to believe that he could succeed without a wholehearted acceptance of the authority of divine revelation.

Such an acceptance is exceedingly difficult to make. To do so is to shift the source of authority from ourselves to God. As sinful persons we unconsciously attribute final authority to ourselves. We soon learn that we are not intuitive experts in the areas of chemistry, architecture, thermodynamics, or similar fields. But every one of us, by nature, believes he is an absolute expert in the truths of religion.

There are at least three wrong responses which we make to the revelation of God. We reject it, we resist it, and we pervert it. Even in the life of the committed Christian these three may be present at one time. Although such an individual may submit to divine authority in many areas of daily life, he will, in some areas, reject the will of God, perhaps almost unconsciously so; in others he will accept it partially, with resistance; and in other areas he will attempt to succeed with a perversion of divine revelation.

Such a sinful response is intensified in the life of the non-Christian. It is not unusual for such a person to glibly call God "a liar" (I John 5:10). In Scripture God has said that all men are unrighteous and sinners (Rom. 3:10, 23), but the non-Christian states, "I'm not a sinner!" God has said that no man may come to Him except through Jesus Christ (John 14:6) and by the avenue of the new birth (John 3:3, 5), but the non-Christian affirms, "I don't need to believe in anyone but myself and I'll get there by my good works!"

There is only one correct response to divine authority. It is that of total acceptance. In the inner spiritual life it means complete surrender. In the manifestation of spiritual life it means complete obedience. It is surrender and obedience to a person. (See Diagram 4.)

The scriptural foundation: Jesus Christ, His work, and His Word.

God is final authority. And in Christianity we are dealing with God, not with a man, an institution, an experience, a way of thinking, or even a way of life.

The authority in Christianity is reflected in its three foundation stones. These form the minimal content of the gospel. The apostle Paul stated that the gospel had to do with (1) Jesus Christ, (2) His death, burial, and resurrection, and (3) Scripture

21

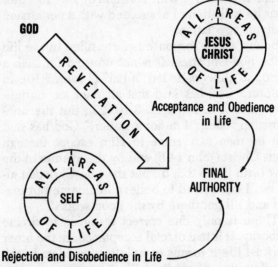

GOD

REVELATION

ALL AREAS OF LIFE

JESUS CHRIST

Acceptance and Obedience in Life

FINAL AUTHORITY

ALL AREAS OF LIFE

SELF

Rejection and Disobedience in Life

Diagram 4. *The key to success:* Accept the revelation of God as your final authority and in your obedience give Jesus Christ His rightful place. Cancel out your sinful self.

(I Cor. 15:1-4). The same threefold emphasis is found in the post-resurrection instruction of our Lord (Luke 24:44-48).

The authority of God is vested first of all in Jesus Christ. He is, according to Scripture, the eternal Son of God. Out of love He became a member of the human race to be man's Redeemer.

The Lord Jesus Christ declared that He was the truth (John 14:6) and the apostle Paul stated that all wisdom and knowledge finds its source in Him (Col. 2:3). The authority of God therefore rests in a person. We may not ". . . refuse him that speaketh" (Heb. 12:25). Without Him we can do nothing (John 15:5).

Genuine Christianity is a manifestation of God in human history. The nature, characteristics, and structure of Christianity has been determined by who and what God is. God is holy. We have been commanded to be holy (I Peter 1:15, 16). God is love. We have been commanded to love one another as we have been loved (John 13:34). The list is quite endless. God has revealed Himself. When this revelation is correctly practiced, the result is biblical Christianity.

The authority in Christianity is also found in the redemptive work of the Lord Jesus. His work may be described as the deeds of God in history. Those deeds determine the structure of Christianity.

An illustration of this is found in the Old Testament. There we are told how God supernaturally delivered His people through the events described as the exodus. This deed of God formed the basis as well as the structure of the theocracy. The Hebrew people were therefore a redeemed race. They belonged to God. The yearly memorial of the passover was to remind them of these truths. The very roots of their nation, their calling, and their religion were found in the exodus.

Biblical Christianity has been unalterably structured by the incarnation of Jesus Christ, from His life and ministry, from His crucifixion, His resurrection, the ascension, and from Pentecost. When the Christian sins, acting as though he belonged to himself, he is acting out of harmony with the character and deeds of God. Sin is therefore described in the Bible as "lawlessness" (I John 3:4). This is to emphasize that it is a violation or contradiction of authority. To sin against God is to act contrary to His nature and contrary to the deeds of God in history.

Since the authority in biblical Christianity is found in the work of Christ, it is necessary for the Christian to accept the evaluation and the demands of these deeds. Christ died to deliver us from the guilt and power of sin. The only correct response we may make is to accept this evaluation of sin. Man is under a solemn authority to repent of sin, to condemn and forsake it in all of its forms, to receive the forgiveness of salvation and the daily deliverance and enablement provided by Jesus Christ for a successful Christian life. The Christian may not live as though Christ did not die and rise from the grave. These deeds have authoritatively structured every facet of biblical Christianity.

The authority in and for Christianity is also found in the Holy Scripture. This does not mean that Scripture is a third type of authority. The three foundation stones of Christianity, the person of Jesus Christ, His deeds in history, and His Word, are inseparably related. God has not only revealed Himself in history but also through the inspired record and interpretation of His work. What we know of God and His work is through His authoritative Word.

When Jesus Christ was on earth He referred to and utilized Scripture as final authority. He spoke of it as "the commandment of God," and as "the Word of God" (Mark 7:8-13). Of His opponents He repeatedly asked, "... Have ye not read ... ?" (Matt. 12:3, 5; 19:4). He quoted Scripture in His temptation (Matt. 4:4, 7, 10) and reminded the disciples that all which had been prophesied of Him would surely come to pass (Luke 18:31).

The Lord Jesus pointed out that it was contradictory indeed to call Him "Lord" and then disobey His Word (Luke 6:46). In harmony with this the Bible teaches the inseparable relationship of love for God and obedience to His Word (John 14:15, 23, 24; I John 2:3-5; 5:3; II John 6). We may not presume that our actions are acceptable with God or that we are expressing love to God while disobeying Scripture. Such an attitude is a violation of the very structure of Christianity.

Christianity comes to us as final authority. It is a manifestation of God's character, which, in turn, has been revealed through the deeds of God in history, and in His inspired Word. (See Diagram 5).

The inescapable results: Spiritual freedom or slavery.

It is not enough to live in harmony with the church, to obey all the rules of the legalist, to perform all the ceremonies of the liturgist, to say all the right words of the Pharisee, to have the right experiences of the emotionalist, and to perform the right services of the Christian worker. We *may* do all these things without commitment, without faith and love, and without serious question as to whether God is dead or alive. We may, indeed, do all these things and be lost.

25

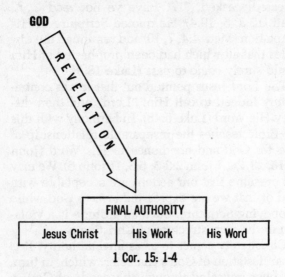

GOD

REVELATION

FINAL AUTHORITY

Jesus Christ	His Work	His Word

1 Cor. 15: 1-4

Diagram 5. *The key to success:* Recognize that the source of authority in biblical Christianity is found in the person of Jesus Christ, in His work, and in His Word.

Christianity demands a complete surrender of one's self to God in the acceptance of His authority. This surrender is a personal subjugation of one's will to Another. The apostle Paul described himself as ". . . a servant of Jesus Christ" (Rom. 1:1).

Christianity has been designed by God to be practiced. Therefore, it must be put into practice before it becomes effective. It is the provision of a *daily* redemption. When we are in total subjection to God and live in daily obedience, the power and grace of biblical Christianity will flow into our life.

Since more will be said about this later it may be sufficient here to point out the biblical nature of this principle. Simply stated it is this: when we obey, God works. This is in no way meant to deny the sovereignty of God nor the depravity of man. All faith and obedience can be traced back only to God's sovereign generosity.

The promise of Jesus Christ is simple and clear. He said, "And ye shall know the truth, and the truth shall make you free" (John 8:32). The word *know* in Scripture designates more than a mere intellectual apprehension. It includes decisions of faith and correct practice. It is self-evident from Scripture and from what has been said before that to "know the truth" is the practice of a personal relationship.

The freedom promised by Christ is primarily spiritual. It is the freedom of the inner man. It is freedom to be the right kind of person, to be able to choose your own thoughts and actions without being pressured by men, circumstances, or sinful desires. It is the freedom produced by the grace and power of God which enables one to know right and wrong, to practice the right, and to enjoy it.

The warning of Jesus Christ is equally clear. He said, ". . . Whosoever committeth sin is the servant of sin" (John 8:34). To "commit sin" is the opposite of "knowing the truth." It is the rejection of the personal authority of Christianity and the elevation of self to the position of God. It is the practice of making one's self the final authority, and personal satisfaction the goal of one's endeavor. When this choice is made and practiced

27

it produces slavery. One becomes enslaved to one's self. Instead of all things revolving around Jesus Christ, they revolve around one's self. Freedom has been lost, selfishness is practiced, and any enjoyment is highly temporary.

The choice is ours and the results are inescapable—freedom or slavery. (See Diagram 6.)

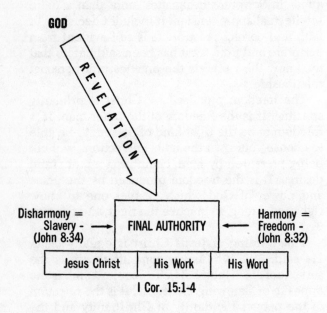

Diagram 6. *The key to success:* Live in harmony with the person of Jesus Christ, the character of His work, and the commandments of His Word. The result will be a glorious freedom.

28

Questions for Discussion

1. Should the Lord Jesus really be our final authority?

2. Are the teachings of the Bible regarding the new birth, repentance, faith, love, sin, and so on, relevant to us today? Why, or why not?

3. Do we as Christians always accept what the Bible has to say?

4. What, in effect, is a non-Christian saying when he says that he is "doing his best" and that he expects to get to heaven by his good works?

5. What are the fundamental cornerstones of Christianity?

6. What did the Lord Jesus declare in John 14:6?

7. How is sin described in the Bible?

8. How is obedience related to our love for God?

9. When do we receive power and grace?

10. What kinds of freedom are promised by the Lord Jesus Christ?

Chapter 3

The Characteristics of Biblical Christianity

Christianity is historical: It is not a myth or legend.

The incarnation of Jesus Christ may not be classed with the mythical birth of Athena who sprang forth fully armed from the head of her father Zeus. The events of the Bible *really happened*. They are historical events!

Christianity traces its source to the revelation of God in history. This revelation cannot be separated from the incarnation of Jesus Christ, His miracles, and, in particular, His resurrection. We have seen that these deeds are not only the basis but also determine the structure of biblical Christianity. If these deeds did not happen historically, then Christianity must be thoroughly and completely rejected.

We are left with no alternative. Scripture is adamant in its demands on this point. This is particularly true of the physical resurrection of Jesus Christ. The resurrection is a part of the ministry of Christ from its very beginning to its end (John 2:18-21; Matt. 20:17-19). When He was pressed to give a sign, He spoke of His resurrection (Matt. 12:38-40). The same is true in the confession of His deity (Matt. 16:13-21; Mark 8:27-31; Luke 9:18-22).

Even the most rudimentary listing of the importance of the resurrection is overwhelming. Scripture frankly states that the resurrection affirms the deity of Jesus Christ (Rom. 1:4); that it is an important evidence for the truthfulness of the gospel (Acts 17:31); that it is an indispensable part of the content of the gospel (Acts 4:2; 17:18; I Cor. 15:1-4, 13-19); that the divine provision of salvation is found in the resurrection (Rom. 4:25; I Peter 1:3); that a confession of belief in the resurrection is a necessity for salvation (Rom. 10:9, 10); that it is the source of the believer's hope of his own resurrection (I Cor. 15:20); that it is the provision of grace and power for the Christian life (Rom. 6:5-14; Phil. 3:10); and that it was the message of the early church (Acts 1:22; 2:22-36; 3:12-19; 5:29-32; 10:34-43; 13:26-41).

Christianity is supernatural: It is not a result of human desire or natural law.

Christianity has not been produced by a wish-fulfilling compulsion of an insecure race. The

31

eternal and infinite God has revealed Himself within the realms of time and space. His activity, therefore, cannot be explained by utilization of natural law. Christianity has within it the element of the miraculous.

This characteristic is an affirmation that God has an existence independent of and separate from His creation. This rejects the view that God and the universe are the same, as held by pantheism, or that God has withdrawn Himself from His creation, as taught by deism.

The supernatural origin of Christianity may be illustrated in the birth and nature of the Jewish religion. Both sacred and secular history testify that Israel worshiped one God (monotheism) when the surrounding nations were worshiping many gods (polytheism). She worshiped a sovereign God, who ruled over all, while her neighbors worshiped gods related to certain sections of land. Her religion was ethically and religiously moral while the religions about Palestine were tainted with immorality. To explain these fundamental differences is very difficult on a naturalistic basis. It is hardly sufficient to refer to Jewish genes and chromosomes.

Christianity is redemptive: It is not mere religious advice.

Christianity purports to be practical and powerfully so. Its leading exponent, the apostle Paul, stated that he was not ashamed of the gospel because it worked (Rom. 1:16). This is why the term *gospel* has generally been designated as "good news."

God has provided in Jesus Christ and His sacrificial death a spiritual deliverance. He has provided life (Eph. 2:5) for our death (Eph. 2:1); forgiveness (Col. 2:13) for our guilt (Rom. 3:23); righteousness (Rom. 8:3, 4) for our unrighteousness (Rom. 3:10); reconciliation (Eph. 2:13-16) for our alienation (Eph. 2:12); and cleansing (I Cor. 6:11) for our depravity (I Cor. 6:9, 10). The list is endless. Why one would reject Christianity when there is so much practical good to be obtained is beyond human logic. It is, in fact, diabolical.

In Scripture the redemptive characteristic of Christianity is portrayed by words such as *grace* and *power*. The former generally indicates the work of Jesus Christ whereby man may be freely accepted by God (John 1:17; Eph. 2:8, 9). The latter usually designates the provision or the effect of God's grace (I Cor. 1:24; Eph. 1:19-23).

Christianity is redemptive because there is a Redeemer. Jesus Christ, the Son of God, fulfilled God's demand in that He bore man's judgment on Calvary (Rom. 5:6-11; II Cor. 5:21; I Peter 2:24). What we deserve fell upon Him. We have been redeemed.

Christianity is representative: It is more than a religious philosophy.

When Jesus Christ became a member of the human race, He did so as man's representative. This is one of the reasons for His baptism and temptation. He acted on behalf of those believers who were given to Him by His Father (John 17:2, 9, 19).

The work of men who have been given the legal right of representation may illustrate this facet of Christianity. Such men may travel to a distant city or country. As the representative of some firm or institution they may sign their name to a great sheaf of orders. In a legal sense the president of the firm is signing his name in his representative. So are the vice-presidents and all who may be involved. What their representative does involves all of them.

And so it is in the work of Jesus Christ. When He lived His righteous life in fulfilment of God's demand, all believers were identified in His obedience (Rom. 5:19; 8:3, 4; 10:3, 4; Gal. 4:4, 5). They were seen by God as living in Christ. Christ not only died for the believer, the believer died in and with Him (Rom. 6:1-8; Gal. 2:20). He was resurrected in and with Christ, he has ascended in and with Christ and is now seated "in the heavenlies" (Eph. 2:5, 6; Col. 3:1-3).

The practical application of this characteristic of Christianity is breath-taking. All the value of the representative work of Jesus Christ has been given to the believer! It has been imputed to him as a free gift. It has been written into his spiritual bank account. This is why the apostle Paul stated that the believer, in Christ, has been blessed with all spiritual blessings (Eph. 1:3), ". . . all things are yours" (I Cor. 3:21).

Christianity is personal: It is not theoretical or abstract.

It is Jesus Christ who stands at the door (Rev. 3:20). He bids no one stand at arm's length.

Christianity not only revolves around Jesus Christ, He is Himself the divine provision for all of man's redemptive needs.

In salvation man receives, through repentance and faith, the person of Jesus Christ, who becomes his Savior (John 1:12; Acts 16:31). Salvation is therefore not so much an experience as it is a relationship with the Son of God.

The same principle holds true in all facets of the Christian life. The apostle Paul described the Lord Jesus as the believer's "wisdom," "power," "righteousness," "sanctification," and "redemption" (I Cor. 1:24, 30). All areas of man's need can be subsumed under these five headings. God has made Himself available to us in and through the person and work of Jesus Christ.

In harmony with this truth Paul sought to "know Him" (Phil. 3:10); and emphasized the importance of being conformed to His image (Rom. 8:28, 29). He spoke of Christ's presence in the believer as "the hope of glory" (Col. 1:27), and prayed that the saints at Ephesus might grow in their "knowledge of him" (Eph. 1:17).

The invitation is clear, "Come unto *me* ... *I* will give you rest" (Matt. 11:28, italics mine).

Christianity is revelatory: It is not an ambiguous guess.

God is not an object which man may subject to his own scrutiny. If God had not chosen to reveal Himself, man would have been left in a religious enigma.

35

That God would make Himself known is beyond man's wildest dream. But it is true.

Christianity is authoritative: It is not a compilation of subjective human opinion.

That God has spoken is an inescapable fact. How to assess such a "speaking" is insurmountably difficult. The word *authoritative* is indeed necessary but woefully weak. No word or concept is adequate here.

The extent of man's depravity is portrayed in his arrogant "ability" to hear and yet reject the revelation of God as irrelevant or even as false and to disobey God with impudent smugness!

Christianity is covenantal: It is not a powerless invitation of dubious promise.

The invitation of salvation and its attendant promises come into the lives of God's elect with irresistible force. Such speaking is accompanied with a life-giving power (John 5:24, 25; Eph. 2:1, 6; Col. 2:13; I Peter 1:3).

As a result, the true believer is brought into a covenantal relationship with God. This is the manifestation of the Father's covenant or promise with the Son in the covenant of redemption (John 17:2, 4, 6-12, 22-26), which was made before time began. The new covenant of this present time (Heb. 8:6-13; 9:15) was anticipated in the Old Testament covenant (Jer. 32:40; 33:19-26). Jesus Christ is the Mediator of the new covenant (Heb. 8:6) and the believer's Surety (Heb. 7:22), so that all the salvation provisions of the new covenant will surely be his (Heb. 8:10-13). The new covenant was initiated or ratified by the work of Jesus Christ in His atonement (Matt. 26:26-28; Heb. 7:11-28; 9:15-28; 10:1-24). One of the purposes in the ordinance of the Lord's Supper is to remind the believer of his covenantal relationship with God (I Cor. 11:23-26).

The true Christian does not belong to himself; he belongs to God. Through the vicarious work of Jesus Christ and the application of this work in divine sovereignty, God has brought the Christian into an eternal covenantal relationship with Himself.

Christianity is exclusive: It is not the highest form of the human religious quest.

Christianity is the result of *divine* revelation. It is a disclosure by God, not a discovery by man.

There is only one way to God. Jesus Christ said, "I am the way . . . no man cometh unto the Father, but by me" (John 14:6).

Christianity is not the most highly developed form of man's search for God. It is not related to such religions as animism and Hinduism as the fruit and flower are related to the seed. Christianity has not been produced by a religious evolutionary force.

While there are elements of truth in all the religions, Christianity stands alone as the truth.

Christianity, we have seen, revolves around the person of Jesus Christ. Every religion, therefore, which does not believe in Jesus Christ as the eternal Son of God and practice His Word can only be condemned as false (Matt. 7:21-29; John 3:36; 8:24; Rom. 10:9, 10; I John 4:1-6; 5:9-13).

To be acceptable to God, one must be more than sincere. He must be both sincere and right (John 4:24)!

Christianity is demanding: It is not a weak, sentimental, permissive avocation.

". . . Give up yourself. . . . Surrender your rights. . . . Lose your life. . . . Follow me!" Such statements break through all attempts to treat Christianity as a tolerant hobby. They summarize Christ's demands for discipleship (Mark 8:34, 35).

The mandate within biblical Christianity is not found primarily in its commandments. It is found in the One around whom all in Christianity revolves—Jesus Christ—and in His love.

To be loved by God is the most demanding, obligatory, inescapable imperative that could ever be conceived. To be so loved means to be recognized as a person by the Creator. It means to be the recipient, in some way, of the evidence of God's love—the giving of His Son (John 3:16; I John 3:16; 4:8-21).

That God would love and give Himself in a voluntary sacrifice brings to all men an unavoidable and all-inclusive demand. It is that we love and give up ourselves to God. It means to recognize Him for who He is and to give Him His rightful place in our lives.

To give up a sin here or there, to relinquish a pleasure, to give money, talent, time, and even one's complete life is quite irrelevant (I Cor. 13). God wants and demands the *person*. He wants you, your heart—not your money or your platitudes (Prov. 3:1, 5, 6; 4:4, 23-26; Matt. 22:37, 38). Once the heart is given, then the commandments find their rightful place. They become the means whereby one's love for God is expressed in daily life (John 14:15, 21, 23; I John 2:5; 5:3; II John 6).

Christianity is contemporaneous: It is not a specimen of an antique religious practice.

Christianity is historical but it may never be relegated to the historical past. The Christian may not worship a first-century God. The true and living God is the great "I am" (John 8:58). He is the same today (Heb. 13:8) and is ever present with His own (Matt. 28:20). God is not bound by time and space.

There is something extremely wrong in asking for "the old-time religion," and "the old-time power." God has nothing "old" to give. He who is the truth, with His life, forgiveness, deliverance, authority, demands, and power, is always in the present tense (Heb. 3:7, 13; 13:8).

Questions for Discussion

1. What does the virgin birth of Christ as narrated in the New Testament have in common with the story of Athena?

2. Of what significance to man is Christ's resurrection?

3. Name some New Testament passages that say that the resurrection of Christ is essential to salvation.

4. How can we describe Christianity?

5. Why was Paul able to so boldly proclaim the gospel?

6. According to the Bible, what is grace?

7. According to the New Testament, which two representative men head up the whole human race?

8. What did Christ's crucifixion do for us?

9. On what terms is our relationship with God?

10. What demands does God make of believers?

Chapter 4

The Application of Biblical Christianity

The important question: How is the Christian related to God?

Christianity, we have seen, revolves around the person of Jesus Christ. We are not told in Scripture to believe in the church, nor in our good works, nor in baptism or the Lord's Supper. We are to believe in Jesus Christ.

Because of who Jesus Christ is and because of what He has done for us in His death, we are commanded to repent of our sins and to believe in Him as our Lord and Savior (Luke 13:3; 24:46, 47; Acts 26:20; Rom. 10:9, 10; I John 3:23). This is the most important decision one may make. Without it one is still under the condemnation of God (John 3:18, 36); he will be rejected by Christ (Matt. 7:21-29; John 8:24); and be eternally lost (Rev. 20:11-15).

"Believe on the Lord Jesus Christ, and thou shalt be saved ..." is the promise of God (Acts 16:31).

When we obey God and believe on Jesus Christ as Lord and Savior, Scripture describes our condition by words such as *saved, adoption, begotten, redeemed, forgiven,* and *justified* (Eph. 2:8; 1:5; I Peter 1:3, 18; Col. 2:13; Rom. 5:1).

These words signify a standing before God. They indicate a spiritual position, a relationship which has been obtained for the believer by Jesus Christ through His death. The believer is seen as having received the benefits of the work of Jesus Christ. The value of Christ's work has been imputed to him and he is therefore "saved," "adopted," "begotten," etc., and brought into the relationship of salvation (Rom. 5:1-11; 8:31-39; Eph. 1:3-14; Col. 2:10-15; I Peter 1:1-5; I John 5:9-13).

The Scripture describes all believers, therefore, as "complete" (Col. 2:10). In the Greek, in which the New Testament was written, this word means "possess fully" and the grammatical construction indicated a finished product.

To explain what he meant in calling the Christian "complete," the apostle Paul indicated that the believer in Jesus Christ "fully possessed" at least five things.

He has received a spiritual cleansing (Col. 2:11). This means that the moral uncleanness which characterizes every non-believer (Isa. 64:6) has been washed away. The believer, even though he may feel unclean, has been cleansed (I Cor. 6:11).

The Christian, as "complete," has been "quickened" by God (Col. 2:13). The word *quickened* means "to make alive." This teaches the great truth that God has given eternal life to all who believe on His Son (John 3:16, 36; I John 5:11, 12). Though once dead to God (Eph. 2:1), the believer now possesses life (John 10:28) and has experienced the new birth (John 3:3, 5).

The third possession of the Christian is forgiveness (Col. 2:13). The Bible, by use of the word "all" emphasizes the universality of this forgiveness. This pertains to man's guilt (Rom. 3:23) with its resultant condemnation (John 3:18) and death (Rom. 5:12; 6:23). The believer is fully forgiven; he is no longer guilty, no longer under the sentence of condemnation and death (John 5:24; Rom. 8:1).

The believer has also been justified (Col. 2:14). As man's representative, Jesus Christ satisfied the demands of God's law. This work has been imputed to the believer. On this basis the believer is looked upon by God as justified, i.e., as though he had perfectly obeyed God and was therefore perfectly righteous (Rom. 5:1, 19; 8:1-4; 10:3, 4).

The final possession, which Paul indicates as belonging to every Christian, is that of freedom from Satan (Col. 2:15). Christ came into our nature to free us from the enemy (Heb. 2:14, 15; I John 3:8). The value and power of His work has been imputed to us. The believer has been set free (Eph. 1:19—2:6; Col. 1:13). He no longer belongs to Satan—he belongs to God and irrevocably so.

The remarkable factor here is that the believer possesses all of these spiritual benefits completely. He is not half forgiven or half justified. This is what Paul meant by "complete." The believer "fully possesses" all of these benefits.

In sharp contrast the Bible exhorts the believer to "seek," "mortify," "put off," and to "put on" (Eph. 4:24; Col. 3:1, 5, 8). There are many commandments which specify that the Christian is to "grow" (I Peter 2:2; II Peter 3:18), and to "work out your own salvation" (Phil. 2:12).

Scripture, therefore, addresses the Christian in a twofold manner. On one hand it instructs him in the permanence of his possession of salvation into which he has been fully brought. On the other hand it exhorts him to develop his "walk" and his "witness." In the former area he is reminded that he is "complete" and in the latter he is always "incomplete."

The instruction in all of this is to the effect that the believer has a twofold relationship with God— the relationship of salvation, in which he is complete, and the relationship of sanctification, in which the believer will always be incomplete. (See Diagram 7.)

The necessary distinction: How is salvation related to sanctification?

In order to understand the Bible and to live successfully, we must clearly distinguish between our salvation and our sanctification. To confuse the two will bring uncertainty and ambiguity into all aspects of life and thought.

This distinction is necessary in order to understand the plan of salvation. The Bible is adamant

44

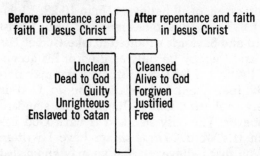

Before repentance and faith in Jesus Christ

After repentance and faith in Jesus Christ

Unclean
Dead to God
Guilty
Unrighteous
Enslaved to Satan

Cleansed
Alive to God
Forgiven
Justified
Free

Diagram 7. *The key to success:* Accept the Word of God as your final authority. Believe *God,* not your feelings or circumstances! If you have repented and believed in Jesus Christ as Savior and Lord, you *are* complete in Him.

in its denial that salvation is based on good works. It emphasizes in a great variety of ways that one does not achieve salvation by human endeavor of any type (Matt. 7:21-23; Luke 18:9-14; Gal. 2:16; 3:11; Eph. 2:8, 9). Salvation is the gift of God (Rom. 6:23) and is received by faith (John 3:36; Eph. 2:8, 9; I John 5:9-13).

It is also necessary to make this distinction in order to live the Christian life successfully. Salvation may be likened to the foundation on which the Christian life is built as a superstructure. To believe that the foundation is defective, that it must continually be shored up, and that it is in constant danger of disappearing altogether would thoroughly discourage even the most committed Christian.

The Bible is emphatically clear on this point. God has promised to give eternal life to all who believe (John 1:12; 3:36). This life, or salvation, with all the benefits described earlier, is the present possession of all believers (John 10:28; I John 5:11, 12). The one who has received Jesus Christ as Lord and Savior is exhorted to take God at His Word and thereby be fully assured of his acceptance by God (I John 5:9-13). How we may personally feel about our relationship to God is entirely irrelevant. Our feelings are no standard whatsoever. The only standard is what God has said in His Word. *"These things* have I written unto you that believe . . . that ye may *know* that ye have eternal life . . ."* (I John 5:13, italics mine).

At this point many earnest Christians confuse the witness of the Holy Spirit and their feelings. They believe, when they lose their "feeling" of assurance, that they have lost the witness of the Holy Spirit. The only conclusion they can draw is that they are not true believers. It is very important for us to recognize that the witness of the Holy Spirit is not our feeling. The "witness" is the Holy Spirit's instruction to us that God has authoritatively spoken in His Word (John 14:26; 15:26; 16:13-15; Rom. 8:15, 16; Gal. 4:6; I John 5:9-13). The Holy Spirit has not been sent to make the believer "feel" that he is a Christian. He was sent to bear witness to Jesus Christ and the Scripture and on that basis to lead the believer into the assurance of salvation. Therefore, the Holy Spirit "witnesses" within the believer that the Scripture is true.

To doubt God's Word and work because of personal feeling is a very dishonoring thing to do. God is truth. He is the sovereign Lord. He is worthy of all trust and confidence. He has given us His Word. We must accept His Word, believe what He has said about us and our salvation, and obey His commandments. When we do so we are co-operating with the Holy Spirit.

Having recognized that the salvation foundation of our life is complete and permanent, we may then confidently assume responsibility for the superstructure.

The biblical description: The characteristics of salvation and sanctification.

In salvation the Christian has a "standing" before God which is complete (Col. 2:10). In contrast, the daily life of sanctification is not complete and may be described as his "state." The believer's "standing" is based on the divine work of imputation. That is, God simply gives the believing sinner all the salvation benefits purchased for him by Jesus Christ. The believer's "state" is based on the divine work of impartation. Here God continually gives to the believer those virtues and enablements which he is spiritually able to receive and practice.

The first characteristic which enables one to distinguish between salvation and sanctification is that the former is a gift while the latter must be claimed. The benefits of salvation, some of which have been listed earlier, are freely given to all who believe on Jesus Christ as Lord and Savior. They cannot be purchased, or merited, nor are they the product of some natural endowment or

47

heritage. They can only be personally received (Rom. 6:23; Eph. 2:8, 9).

In contrast to the benefits of salvation, those of sanctification must be claimed. We receive such virtues and abilities only as we learn how to put them into practice by faith and love (Rom. 6:16; I Peter 1:22). An illustration of such a benefit would be the ability to resist temptation. We grow in this ability by truly desiring it, by claiming the provision and promise of God (I Cor. 10:13), and then by making use of it in acts of faith (Matt. 4:3-11; Heb. 2:14-18; James 1:2, 12-14; I Peter 1:6, 7; II Peter 2:9).

The second characteristic indicates that the benefits of salvation admit of no degrees while the benefits of sanctification, by contrast, do admit of degrees, such a benefit of salvation as forgiveness, is fully given by God. To possess forgiveness at all, in the area of salvation, is to possess it fully (Col. 2:13; Heb. 10:17). All believers possess forgiveness in the same degree—completely. This is also true for justification, eternal life, adoption, and all such benefits.

That which the believer possesses by way of sanctification is never complete. Whatever the benefit may be, it is only partially known and utilized. One Christian may possess the ability to resist temptation only in a very small degree while another may possess it in a much larger degree. All Christians have some ability to resist temptation, but all in a different degree.

The third characteristic distinction between the provisions of salvation and sanctification is that the former are permanent and the latter may be transitory. The provisions of salvation are, happily, permanent. We receive these benefits as a gift, they admit of no degrees, and they are ours permanently. This comforting truth is implied in the type of life which God gives to those who believe: it is "eternal" life. Jesus Christ said, "and I give unto them eternal life; and they shall never perish ..." (John 10:28). We do not merit these benefits of salvation nor do we keep them by merit.

By comparison, the virtues and abilities of sanctification are not necessarily permanent. It is very possible to attain a high degree of progress in some area of Christian practice and then to lose it through neglect. It is debatable whether one may lose any benefit of sanctification absolutely. Undoubtedly this would not be true. Every Christian, however, has experienced remarkable growth in some area only to find a stunting of that growth and a decline in ability due to carelessness (I Cor. 3:1-4; 5:1-13; 6:1-8; 11:18-22; II Thess. 3:6-15; II Tim. 4:10).

The fourth characteristic which distinguishes between the benefits of salvation and sanctification has to do with their source. The benefits of salvation depend only on the person and work of Jesus Christ. Through His representative work, which has been considered earlier, He obtained all the provisions of salvation. These are given to all who believe as a gift. They do not vary in degrees; they are ours permanently, and they depend only on Jesus Christ (Rom. 3:20-31; 5:6-11; 8:1-4, 31-39; Phil. 1:6).

In sharp contrast, the benefits of sanctification depend not only on Jesus Christ and His work, but *also* upon the spiritual cooperation of the believer. It has been pointed out earlier that one must desire and learn how to utilize these benefits. The provision has been made by Jesus Christ so that His people may live successfully. The Holy Spirit has been sent to teach and anoint the believer. But it is clear from Scripture and from the experience of every Christian that our cooperation is necessary.

When we desire to obey God, learn how to submit to His authority, and how to put the Bible into daily practice, then the grace and power of God

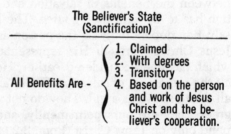

The Believer's Standing
(Salvation)

All Benefits Are -
1. A gift
2. Without degrees
3. Permanent
4. Based only on the Person and work of Jesus Christ

The Believer's State
(Sanctification)

All Benefits Are -
1. Claimed
2. With degrees
3. Transitory
4. Based on the person and work of Jesus Christ and the believer's cooperation.

Diagram 8. *The key to success:* Do not confuse your relationship with God in salvation which is complete and your relationship with God in sanctification which will never be complete in this life.

50

will flow into our lives. "But God be thanked, that ye were the servants of sin, but ye have obeyed from the heart that form of doctrine which was delivered you. Being then made free from sin, ye became the servants of righteousness" (Rom. 6:17, 18). (See Diagram 8.)

Questions for Discussion

1. When is a person assured of a perfect standing before God?

2. According to the New Testament, what does being "complete" in Christ mean?

3. What does Paul mean when he speaks of a person being "quickened"?

4. What does the word *justified* mean in Scripture?

5. How is a person sanctified?

6. On what does our assurance of salvation depend?

7. What is the function of the Holy Spirit?

8. On what does a believer's standing before God depend?

9. Which of the following—salvation, sanctification, justification, adoption—allows for degrees or stages of development?

10. What happens when a believer begins to neglect his sanctification?

Chapter 5

The Biblical Provision for Sanctification

The practical question: Is sanctification an experience, a relationship, or a person?

The answer to this practical question is that sanctification is all three, but in the reverse order. Primarily, sanctification finds its source in the person of Jesus Christ. *He* has been made our "sanctification" (I Cor. 1:30).

No Christian can cleanse himself from sin and no Christian can produce holiness entirely by his own effort. Only God through His grace can do that. Many earnest Christians have met with great frustration and disappointment in attempting, through a lack of understanding, to sanctify themselves.

This in no way may be taken as an excuse to live a careless, carnal, indifferent Christian life. The believer is under the solemn obligation to live free from sin by learning how to go to God in confession for cleansing and to live in holiness of life by learning how to make decisions of faith in appropriating the person and work of Jesus Christ.

When these two interrelated truths are learned and practiced, then He who is our sanctification will fulfill His will ". . . even your sanctification . . ." (I Thess. 4:3).

Holiness in daily life is not produced, therefore, by resolutions, self-discipline, or any clenching-of-the-teeth attitude alone. Determination and committal are important but are not enough. Holiness is produced by God through His grace.

Sanctification is therefore the result of a relationship. When Jesus Christ, our sanctification, is given His rightful place in our life, the effect of His presence and grace will be evident.

Sanctification is not automatic. The daily life of many Christians testifies to that. It is also evident that sanctification is not a once-for-all decision. It was shown earlier that the benefits of sanctification must be claimed, they are possessed in a variety of degrees, they are transitory benefits, and they also depend on our cooperation with God. To summarize, this would indicate that sanctification is progressive. Our growth in grace is a daily matter. The basic issues of the Christian life must be maintained by daily decisions.

What are the daily decisions which we must make? Christianity, we have seen, is demanding. We have been commanded to surrender ourselves to God. The issue is not our money, time, pleasures, or even our sins. We are to surrender ourselves as a living sacrifice (Mark 8:34; Rom. 12:1).

Sanctification does not pertain primarily to our money or sins. It has to do with the person who spends the money and commits the sins. It is the person who is in need.

We are to surrender ourselves to God, not to the church, nor to Christian service, nor to a certain way of life. We have been commanded to give the control, the authority, the rule of our persons to Another. It is not enough to mouth a few words and to shed a few tears.

This surrender to God is the most important decision in progressive sanctification. Many Christians have surrendered only superficially. They have made a hasty, shallow, partial surrender and have been deceived as a result. In such cases a Christian may give up some particular sin or habit, he may yield a certain area of his life to God, may accept some activity of his church as important, or he may resolve to live a better life. All of this is important but irrelevant to the basic issue. The biblical command is inescapable. There is no substitute for the total surrender of the self.

To be a sinner means to be one's own authority. It means to arrogate to ourselves the position of God. This must be recognized, confessed, and reversed. We may no longer play God in our own lives or the lives of others. For sanctification to be meaningful in our life it must grow out of a relationship with Jesus Christ. This relationship is rooted and grounded only in a complete and honest surrender.

Once this decision has been correctly made it must be maintained on a daily basis. The relationship must now be translated into a daily practice.

To surrender ourselves to God means not only that we give Him the control of our inner life, but that all areas of life must be recognized as belonging to Him. Our surrender to Him must be maintained in our motives, ambitions, pleasures, thoughts, evaluations, beliefs, and activities. This is why daily decisions which acknowledge divine Lordship are so important.

And now it is evident that sanctification is also an *experience*. One must accept the authority of God as He has spoken in His Word and learn how to put the Bible into practice in daily life. Sanctification must be a part of our total experience.

This does not mean that we become enslaved to rules. The opposite is true. The Christian who has surrendered Himself to God and has learned to practice the principles of sanctification is under servitude only to God. He is free. This, on the other hand, does not make him irresponsible to the Bible, the church, Christian service, and the needs and feelings of others. In all these ways he will learn to express his love to God. Love for God and obedience to the Word of God, as we have seen, are inseparable (John 14:15; I John 5:3). (See Diagram 9.)

The doctrinal question: How is sanctification related to the work of Christ?

Every benefit of the gospel, including sanctification, has been provided for the Christian by Jesus Christ through His crucifixion, resurrection, ascension, and the sending of the Holy Spirit on the day of Pentecost.

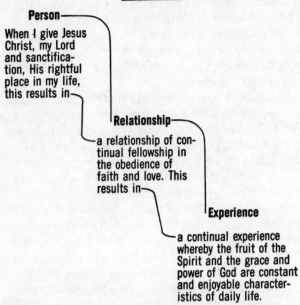

Person—

When I give Jesus Christ, my Lord and sanctification, His rightful place in my life, this results in—

Relationship—

a relationship of continual fellowship in the obedience of faith and love. This results in—

Experience

a continual experience whereby the fruit of the Spirit and the grace and power of God are constant and enjoyable characteristics of daily life.

Diagram 9. *The key to success:* is a person—Jesus Christ.

It is important to understand that, in each of these historical deeds, Christ provided for more than the believer's initial salvation.

In the crucifixion the believer has been justified, delivered from condemnation, and reconciled to God (Rom. 5:6-11). All of this applies to the gift of salvation. Jesus Christ died as the believer's substitute. He took upon Himself the condemnation and judgment which had been justly passed on mankind. He died under the wrath of

God so that the believer may never experience that wrath. Redemption has been obtained. There is a complete, legal forgiveness of sins (Eph. 1:7; Col. 2:13; Heb. 10:17).

However, Jesus Christ died not only that man may be redeemed; He died that the believer also may be able to live a successful Christian life. And this is what Scripture calls "sanctification."

In His crucifixion, Jesus Christ has provided a cleansing from the power, influence, and effect of the believer's sinful nature. This nature is called the "flesh" in Scripture (Rom. 7:18-25; 8:12-14). In His death, as the believer's representative, Jesus Christ brought the fallen nature of man under the judgment of God (Rom. 6:6). A cleansing has therefore been secured, so that the believer may be free from the sinful patterns of life which he yet possesses and which is the source of so much of his spiritual defeat (Rom. 6:6-22).

In Scripture some aspects of both salvation and sanctification are also related to the resurrection of Jesus Christ.

In regard to salvation, the believer's justification (Rom. 4:25), spiritual birth (I Peter 1:3), and future resurrection (I Cor. 15:20-58) are shown to have their source in Christ's resurrection.

The sanctification benefits of the resurrection are also clearly stated in Scripture. The apostle Paul spoke of his desire to experience the power of the resurrection in daily life (Phil. 3:10). And he prayed for the Christians at Ephesus that they would know this same power (Eph. 1:19, 20). What Paul is referring to is the enablement which Christ provided through His resurrection so that the believer may live with spiritual virtue, grace, and power in his life. This is described in the Bible as being "... alive unto God ..." (Rom. 6:11).

The believer, therefore, need not live with doubt in his life. He may have, through Christ's resurrection, the virtue of faith. Instead of pessimism and discouragement, he may have hope. And instead of bitterness, estrangement, and selfishness, he may have love (I Cor. 13; I Thess. 1:3). Again the list of practical benefits is endless (Gal. 5:22, 23; Eph. 4:22-32; Phil. 4:5-8; Col. 3:10-17).

To the ascension of Jesus Christ the Bible also attributes some benefits of both salvation and sanctification.

In the area of salvation Jesus Christ ascended into heaven to be the believer's forerunner (Heb. 6:19, 20) and intercessor (Heb. 7:25; 8:1; 9:24). The apostle Paul also indicated that the believer has been given the position of legal authority over Satan by means of Christ's ascension (Eph. 1:19-23). He is "seated in the heavenlies" with Jesus Christ (Eph. 2:5, 6).

This position of authority provides daily *deliverance* from Satan. This deliverance must now be put into practice in the believer's sanctification. He is commanded to guard against allowing Satan some sinful opportunity in his life (Eph. 4:27) and to deliberately appropriate all the benefits of his relationship with Christ so he may be able to resist the devil (Eph. 6:10-18; I Peter 5:8, 9). The Christian has not only been crucified in and with Christ (Gal. 2:20); he has been raised from the grave and has ascended in the person of His representative (Eph. 2:5, 6; Col. 3:1-3). The spiritual benefits of this position, when practiced by the Christian, are a part of his progressive sanctification.

On the Day of Pentecost the ascended Lord Jesus Christ bestowed the Holy Spirit on all those who were believers (Acts 2:33). In a similar way to the other three deeds of atonement, the believer has a twofold relationship to the person and work of the Holy Spirit.

It is the Holy Spirit who convicts the non-Christian of his sinful and lost condition (John 16:7-11). He brings the convicted person into the benefits of the new birth through the gift of repentance and faith (John 3:3-5; II Thess. 2:13; I Peter 1:2). The Holy Spirit protects and preserves the new believer as His indwelling "seal" (II Cor. 1:22; Eph. 1:13, 14; 4:30) and makes him a member of the "body of Christ" (Rom. 8:9; I Cor. 12:13). The believer becomes the "temple" of the Holy Spirit (I Cor. 3:16, 17; 6:19).

As related to sanctification the Holy Spirit resides in the believer to be his "Comforter" (Helper) in a continual *anointing* (John 14:16, 17, 26; 15:26; 16:13, 14). While Jesus Christ is the believer's Sanctification, it is the Holy Spirit who is his Sanctifier. The Spirit leads the believer in progressive freedom from the sinfulness of his fallen nature (Rom. 8:13; Gal. 5:16-18) through an increasing understanding of Scripture and applying it to his daily life (I Peter 1:22). The Holy Spirit witnesses to the believer concerning the authenticity of the Word of God and assures him on that basis of his relationship to God (Rom. 8:15, 16; Gal. 4:5, 6; I John 5:9-13). He undergirds the Christian in his prayer life (Rom. 8:26, 27) and gives him spiritual

59

	Crucifixion	Resurrection	Ascension	Pentecost
Salvation	Reconciliation to God	Spiritual rebirth	Representation in heaven. Legal deliverance from Satan.	The baptizing and sealing work of the Holy Spirit
Sanctification	Continual cleansing from the "flesh".	Continual enablement to live in newness of life	Continual freedom from satanic influence	Continual anointing to live and serve God

Diagram 10. *The key to success:* is to understand that sanctification is rooted in the deeds of God in history as well as salvation.

60

gifts so that he might adequately serve God (Rom. 12:3-8; I Cor. 12:1-11; Eph. 4:7-16).

The Christian is commanded not to grieve or quench the Holy Spirit by resisting His leading (Eph. 4:30; I Thess. 5:19) but to be constantly filled with the Spirit through daily obedience (Eph. 5:18).

In summary, then, Jesus Christ, through His atonement, has made an adequate spiritual provision for every area of the believer's daily life. He has provided a daily cleansing through His crucifixion, a daily enablement through His resurrection, a daily deliverance through His ascension, and a daily anointing through Pentecost. It is very important for the Christian to understand this.

The Christian who lives and prays in ambiguity is doomed to failure and disappointment in daily life. (See Diagram 10.)

Questions for Discussion

1. We have just set forth sanctification as an experience, a relationship, and a person. In logical order, which of these is first?

2. If Christ is "made unto us sanctification," what part, if any, must we play in our sanctification?

3. How is holiness produced?

4. What must we daily surrender to God in order to be sanctified?

5. How do we surrender ourselves to God?

6. Is a partial surrender to God better than none at all?

7. According to Scripture, what is the "old man," the "flesh"?

8. To which of these events—crucifixion, resurrection, ascension, second coming—is the intercessory work of the Lord Jesus on the believer's behalf connected?

9. What does Scripture mean when it says the believer in Christ is seated with Him in the heavenlies?

10. How should a believer regard his body?

Chapter 6

The Crucifixion in the Believer's Daily Life

The Crucifixion: The old nature and the need of cleansing.

The believer has been delivered once for all from the guilt of his sin—that is salvation. Now he needs to be progressively delivered from the power of sin—that is sanctification.

To be successful Christians we must recognize our problems, understand them, and learn to overcome them. The first and most formidable problem which stands in the Christian's path of success is himself.

The Christian is a holy and yet sinful person. He not only commits sins; he has an inner "law of sin," which may be described as an evil behavior pattern—primarily self-centeredness. The committing of sins is only the superficial evidence of this underlying pattern. And this is where the problem lies—not with the deeds but with their cause and source. The Christian needs a deliverance, a cleansing, from the "flesh" which is inseparable from himself.

But to acknowledge that we are at fault presents an almost insurmountable problem. It is exceedingly difficult for the believer to confess that he is in need of help. It is far easier to blame failures on a lack of time, money, education, background, intelligence, or personality. It is far easier to place the blame on parents, fellow-workers, roommates, wife or husband, pastor, or even God! Our sinful pride is often much more important and valuable to us than the glory of God and our personal success as Christians.

"Now don't blame that on me; I'm a person of spiritual integrity," is more often heard and implied than, "I was at fault," "I'm sorry I said that," "I need your forgiveness," or, "I am a sinful person and need help."

To be cleansed from my pride, lust, envy, jealousy, covetousness, dishonesty, and bigotry I must acknowledge and confess that I am a proud person, a lustful person, an envious person, a jealous person, a covetous person, a dishonest person, a bigot. This confession must be genuine. It must be more than words. It must be a truthful appraisal in the presence of God.

The way in which we begin with ourselves is to admit and confess that we need the cleansing God has promised (I John 1:9). We must open up our persons to God and allow Him to deal with us. This is absolutely necessary.

First of all, the Christian needs a divine cleansing from the power of this inner law of sin because of what it is. He has an inner pattern of self-centeredness which is at enmity with God (Rom. 8:7). The seriousness of this and its far-reaching effects cannot be overemphasized. The Christian must face the inescapable truth that he belongs to God and must obey God, yet he possesses a sinful pattern of life which is thoroughly antagonistic to all that is holy and loving and true. He has a built-in hindrance to any genuine progress in the Christian life. He may often approve of lust but not purity, of pride but not humility—the list is endless.

It is not easy for the Christian to admit this sinfulness. The Bible, however, is clear on this point (Jer. 17:9; Rom. 1:19-32; 3:10-18) and so is our daily experience, if we are willing to look. We must admit that our first reaction to a new truth from the Scripture is often one of resistance. It is much easier to find ten reasons why we should not obey God than simply to obey. Give the ordinary Christian five seconds and he can rationalize almost any of his vices into virtues!

Because of this law of sin and its warfare against God, the non-Christian is described as an enemy of God (Rom. 5:10). Even in the Christian this pattern of evil continues its opposition to God and therefore to the believer's spiritual progress. No wonder the Christian catches himself disliking God! How quickly and easily he can sit in judgment on God and refuse to accept some teaching of the Bible because of personal disapproval!

Such a description is in no way intended to imply that man is as bad as he can be nor that man cannot do civil good or approve of the good. This,

65

however, is not to be traced to man's goodness but to the common and special grace of God.

This law of sin, the "flesh," cannot be brought under subjugation to the will of God (Rom. 8:7). No amount of prayer, Bible study, decisions of faith, self-discipline, church attendance, and Christian service will change it. What the Christian must do is to learn not to obey his sinful flesh. The Scripture is very clear on this point. The command is not to change the old patterns but to reject them (Eph. 4:22; Col. 3:5-9).

The second reason why the Christian needs to be cleansed is because of what the old patterns do. The Lord Jesus taught His disciples that one was defiled by what came out of man and not by that which went in (Mark 7:17-23). When we accept the prompting of our flesh and put the suggestion into practice, the result is an action or activity out of harmony with the will of God. This expressing of sin is what defiles us. The tragic products of such choices are not only clearly seen in the Bible (Mark 7:21, 22; Rom. 1:21-32; Gal. 5:19-21) but, in some measure, also in the lives of all Christians. Our pride, hypocrisy, jealousy, deceit, selfishness, and lust are easily discernible. So is our lack of love, faith, and hope.

Augustine emphasized the biblical principle that the judgment for sin is inexorably connected with the sin itself (*Confessions*, Book I, par. 19). When sin is committed, the sinner, whether Christian or non-Christian, becomes directly influenced by the sin. Our character is changed by our deliberate choice to disobey God and to practice evil. We become characterized by the nature of our sin! Therefore, in the Bible, the one who steals is described as a "thief," the one who is immoral is an "adulterer," and the one who gossips is a "tale-bearer." When we choose to obey the flesh, the resultant activity will "enslave" us (John 8:34; 1 Rom. 7:15-18, 23, 24).

A third reason why the Christian should learn how to appropriate the divine provision for his flesh is because of what it does not do. It is never a help in the Christian life. Not one victory, not one genuine desire for God, not one holy or loving thought or activity can be traced back to the flesh (Rom. 7:18, 23). This alone should be reason enough for the Christian to seek how he may live in freedom.

A final reason why the earnest believer must give heed to what the Scripture states about his daily life is because of the commandment of God. The Christian has been commanded to "put off . . . the old man" (Eph. 4:22).

This leaves us with no correct alternative but that of obedience. The Christian, therefore, may not live in unconcern about the manifestation of sin in his life. God must be obeyed.

The crucifixion: The fleshly law of sin and the provision for cleansing.

If it is true that the Christian possesses an inner pattern of sinfulness which is at enmity with God, which cannot be brought into subjection to the will of God, which defiles and enslaves, which is never the source of spiritual help, and which he has been commanded by God to reject, then the Christian must seek to understand the provision God has made and to practice it.

In the crucifixion such a provision for cleansing from the power of sin has been made (Rom. 6:1-10). The apostle Paul affirms that the sinful nature, once possessed by every believer, has been judged in the death of Jesus Christ. Acting as our representative, Christ took our nature to His cross so that we may be free from its influence. In His death the "old man" was stripped of its power.

It is important for us to understand that we were identified with Jesus Christ in His death. "I am crucified with Christ . . ." may not only be said by the apostle Paul but by every believer (Gal. 2:20). We were there when our Lord was crucified and we were crucified in and with Him (Rom. 6:1-10; Col. 2:10-15; 3:1-3).

The value of this deliverance has been imputed to the believer. He is, therefore, described in the Bible as being "dead to sin" (Rom. 6:2, 7; Col. 3:3). The apostle Paul explains this statement in Romans 6. It means to possess freedom from sin (Rom. 6:1-11). His reference here is not to forgiveness but to freedom from the power patterns of the old man.

Every believer possesses this freedom legally. We may not understand this nor manifest this freedom in any large measure in our lives. It is ours, however, simply because we are believers. The law of sin in every believer, our greatest personal hindrance to the success of our Christian life, has been judged by God; it has been stripped of its power, and we have been set free. We were crucified with Jesus Christ.

The crucifixion: The fleshly law of sin and the conditions for cleansing.

What the believer possesses legally he must learn to practice in daily life. It is not enough to have an account in the bank. We must learn to write the check.

God has made a provision for our cleansing. The power of this provision, however, will not flow into our daily life until we understand the conditions for cleansing and choose to practice them.

The apostle Paul states that there are three conditions we must meet. The first revolves around the word *reckon* (Rom. 6:11). This indicates that we must make a decision to act in harmony with and on the basis of the atoning work of Christ. We legally died in and with Jesus Christ. Now we must choose to put into practice the provision and principle of the crucifixion no matter what it may cost.

The second condition is a decision to live free from the demands of sin (Rom. 6:12). There is no deliverance when we choose to live in sin or call it by some other name. No amount of tears, prayer, agony, and spiritual work can substitute for the simple decision to obey God and to forsake the sin.

The third condition is a decision to trust God (Rom. 6:13). This is a deliberate dependence on God for the grace necessary to practice the first two decisions. Here the necessity of biblical faith needs to be emphasized. Sanctification is not brainwashing or wish-fulfillment. It is the work of God in the believer. Without faith it is impossible to please God (Heb. 11:6). These three decisions which form the conditions for our cleansing are all decisions of faith.

The important question now is how to apply these three decisions to our daily life. What do they mean in practice?

First of all, we must acknowledge our personal need of divine help. Personal involvement is absolutely necessary. No sinner is ever forgiven until he confesses that he is a sinner and no saint is ever cleansed without acknowledgment of personal need. We must accept what God has said about our fleshly law of sin (Rom. 7:14-24; 8:7) and assume responsibility to obey the commandment to reject the demands of sin (Eph. 4:22).

The second step in deliverance is the necessity of being specific in confession. The flesh manifests itself in specific sins (Gal. 5:19-21; Col. 3:5-9). These must be recognized and confessed as such to God. To call our sins by any other name and to relate ourselves to them by rationalization instead of by confession will make freedom and cleansing an impossibility! When we have been proud, the only recourse is to point our spiritual finger at that sin and call it "pride." When we have gossiped, we must name it for what it is and confess before God that we are a "gossip." For most Christians this is indeed difficult. Our pride and arrogancy are often much more important than the will and power and glory of God. Without confession, however, there is no cleansing (I John 1:9).

The third step is that of forsaking our sin. Having confessed an activity as sinful, we are left with no alternative but that of thoroughly renouncing the sin. What may an earnest Christian do with his sin but to forsake it? The only thing that would ever be worse than committing a sin would be to continue to practice it once its true nature is known. To confess a sin and then not to forsake it is evidence that our confession was false.

The fourth step is to receive Jesus Christ as the specific cleansing we may need. He is our sanctification (I Cor. 1:30). When we were in need of salvation, we received a person—Jesus Christ—as our Savior. In sanctification the principle is the same (Col. 2:6). He is not only our sanctification in general but also in all those specific areas where sin is committed and where sanctification must therefore be practiced. The cleansing which Jesus Christ has provided is inseparable from His person. This is not only true in salvation but in sanctification. God has promised to cleanse us when we truly confess our sin (I John 1:9). Jesus Christ is our cleansing (Rom. 7:24, 25; Phil. 1:11). It is necessary to be exceedingly specific at this point. "Lord Jesus, I confess that I sinned against You in that act of pride. I am a proud person. I choose to forsake my pride by Your grace. In claiming Your promise I receive You as my cleansing from the sin of pride."

The fifth step is to believe God and to live as a cleansed person. This step, as all the others, is a decision of faith. God has promised to cleanse us from unrighteousness (I John 1:9). Having claimed the promise we must act accordingly. God expects us to take Him at His Word. Any doubt as

71

to whether we have been cleansed is out of harmony with the faithfulness of God and the truthfulness of His Word. When temptation comes we must reaffirm our previous decision. The temptation must be rejected in that the sin has already been confessed, forsaken, and cleansing has been received.

When these steps of sanctification are put into practice, the grace and power of God will flow into our lives. When we obey, God works. This principle of sanctification is found throughout the Bible (Phil. 2:12, 13; I Peter 1:22). Obedience produces freedom from sin and righteousness in daily life (Rom. 6:16-18).

GOD'S PROVISION: the old man was crucified in the death of Jesus Christ.

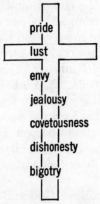

pride
lust
envy
jealousy
covetousness
dishonesty
bigotry

Diagram 11. *The key to success:* Recognize that the old man was crucified in the death of Jesus Christ. Reject all of his sinful characteristics. Receive by faith the cleansing found in Jesus Christ.

72

Only God can deal with sin and only God can produce holiness. The Christian must learn how to make these decisions of faith so the power and grace of the crucifixion may be present in his life. And having made these decisions of faith, he must learn to say no to every facet of sin.

The crucifixion is a historical event. Jesus Christ died to free the believer from the power of his fleshly law of sin. The believer died in Christ. The crucifixion indicated God's disapproval of every form of sin. The believer may not live as though this did not happen. (See Diagram 11.)

Questions for Discussion

1. What should we do when we are at fault about something?

2. Where in the Bible does it say that God is faithful and just to forgive and cleanse sins when they are confessed to Him?

3. What does Jeremiah 17:9 say about the heart?

4. Can the sinful nature of the old man be reformed?

5. Why do Christians need cleansing from the power of the flesh?

6. What role does the Christian play in being rid of the power of the flesh?

7. What does "dead to sin" mean?

8. What are the conditions for cleansing and holy living?

9. Is it necessary to be specific when confessing failure to the Lord Jesus? Why, or why not?

10. What is the basic principle of progressive sanctification?

73

Chapter 7

The Resurrection in the Believer's Daily Life

The resurrection: The new man and the need of enablement.

The provision of cleansing in the crucifixion is largely negative. It is a cleansing from the power of sin. The believer, however, needs more than cleansing. He also needs a divine enablement to obey God and to possess and to practice the virtues commended in the Scripture.

Even the most careless reading of the Bible will indicate the importance of obeying God. Throughout the New Testament, obedience is presented as an evidence of salvation. Those who do not practice the commandments and Word of God are not true believers (I John 2:3-5). Obedience to God is equated with salvation (Heb. 5:9) and forgiveness (I Peter 1:2). In the return of Jesus Christ, those who will be judged are described as those who "know not God, and that obey not the gospel of our Lord Jesus Christ" (II Thess. 1:8).

Even more emphatically, obedience is described as a characteristic of sanctification. To love God is to obey Him (John 14:15, 21, 23; I John 5:3; II John 6). According to Paul and Peter the secret of progressive sanctification is found in the practice of obedience (Rom. 6:16-18; Phil. 2:12, 13; I Peter 1:14-22). The four great exhortations of sanctification, to "put off" (Eph. 4:22; Col. 3:9); "put on" (Eph. 4:24; Col. 3:10); "resist" (Eph. 4:27; 6:11-13; I Peter 5:9); and "be filled" (Eph. 5:18) are amplified and applied throughout the New Testament in principle and precept. There is no substitute nor alternative for obedience.

In regard to sanctification and obedience two things of importance must be kept in mind. The first has to do with motivation. Happy is the person who lives in a culture which demands a morality paralleling the Bible. Not stealing from the neighbor but being kind to him is approved by the Scripture. However, if we refrain from stealing simply because of our culture we are not reflecting sanctification. Even the non-Christian may live according to the demands of culture. Sanctification grows out of a relationship with God—not culture.

It is necessary, therefore, to question our motivation. To act in harmony with the Bible because of our culture, or because of our fear of criticism, or because of our reputation, or because of our desire for success, is surely not an expression of loving obedience to God.

75

The second factor of importance in regard to sanctification concerns one of its characteristics: sanctification is positive. Too often the emphasis is placed upon a negative separation. Many of the commandments of the New Testament do exhort the believer not to engage in certain activities (Eph. 4:25-31; Col. 3:5, 8, 9; I John 2:15-17). This, however, is so we may be free to give God His rightful place in our lives and to practice His will. In the Scripture sanctification is inseparably related to the positive manifestation in daily life of the virtues of love, faith, and hope (Matt. 22:36-40; I Cor. 13; Heb. 11:6; I Thess. 1:3; 3:6; I John 3:14-18). It is not enough to abstain from loving the world (I John 2:15); we must love God (Matt. 22:37, 38). We must do more than refrain from putting faith in ourselves (Jer. 17:5; Luke 18:9); we must put our faith in God (Jer. 17:7; Heb. 11:6; I John 3:23). Freedom from despair and pessimism is not sufficient (Rom. 4:18); one must practice hope in God (Rom. 15:13; I Peter 1:13).

Sanctification is, therefore, a process whereby the believer is increasingly brought into a spiritual conformity with Jesus Christ (Rom. 8:28, 29). For this the Christian needs divine enablement.

The resurrection: The new man and the provision of enablement.

In the New Testament almost all of the positive benefits of salvation and sanctification are traced back to the resurrection of Jesus Christ. In this great deed of God in history, the Lord Jesus Christ not only verified the truthfulness of His divine sonship (Rom. 1:4); presented evidence that His work of atonement was finished and accepted (Acts 13:29-39); assured all men of a future judgment (Acts 17:31) and resurrection (John 5:29; I Cor. 15:20-28; Rev. 20:11-15); but also made adequate provision for the Christian to live in "newness of life" (Rom. 6:4).

In his salvation the believer was given spiritual life (John 3:3, 5; 10:10, 28; 17:2; Eph. 2:5; I John 5:11, 12). Through this work of regeneration his character was transformed and he was given a "new nature" (I Cor. 6:11; II Cor. 5:17; Gal. 6:15). The believer now has the ability, through his new nature, to say no to sin with all its evil, and to live with faith, love, hope, and spiritual power as part of his daily experience. These benefits all find their source in the work of Jesus Christ in His resurrection (Rom. 6:4; 7:4; Col. 2:12, 13; I Peter 1:3, 21).

As the recipient of this work of Christ, the believer is described as being "alive unto God" (Rom. 6:11) and "married to another" (Rom. 7:4). These terms indicate the revolutionary change which has been brought into the life of one who was once dead and alienated from God. They also describe the potential enablement which has been given to every believer.

The apostle Paul explains this provision as a divine power. He prayed for the Ephesian Christians that they might know this power in their daily lives (Eph. 1:19, 20) and stated that he sought to live so he might experience the same enablement (Phil. 3:10).

77

The practical result of this divine provision is that the Christian need no longer live under the dominion of sin. He has been set free and has the ability to live a life of obedience, righteousness, and holiness (Rom. 6:11, 12; Phil. 1:11). Such a life has been described by the apostle Paul as "bring[ing] forth fruit unto God" (Rom. 7:4).

One of the greatest sins and one that is found in the lives of all Christians is our failure to appropriate the provision God has made available through the resurrection. It is not the will of God that we live the Christian life in our own strength. He said, "without me ye can do nothing" (John 15:5).

The Christian stands without excuse before this reality of divine provision.

The resurrection: The new man and the conditions for enablement.

It is one thing to know that Jesus Christ has made an adequate provision for our daily lives but it is quite another to incorporate this provision into our daily practice. What must we do to appropriate this power to live a holy life?

In the crucifixion Jesus Christ provided a cleansing from the believer's sinful flesh. We are therefore exhorted to "put off the old man" (Eph. 4:22; Col. 3:9). In the resurrection Jesus Christ provided an enablement to live a holy life through the provision of a new nature. We are therefore exhorted to "put on the new man" (Eph. 4:24; Col. 3:10). Until we learn to obey God in this way we are doomed to spiritual failure. No amount of pious talk or ambiguous praying can be a substitute for clear-cut decisions of faith.

By the use of the term *new man* the apostle Paul is referring to the new nature and ability which has been given to every believer in his salvation (Phil. 4:13; Col. 1:29; II Peter 1:3, 4). This ability to live the Christian life successfully is not automatic; it must be appropriated by faith. One must learn how to "put on the new man" by deliberate choice and practice.

In the previous chapter we found that the Bible presents three conditions for cleansing. These conditions are to be put into practice through five steps which are all decisions of faith. In regard to the resurrection and the new nature, the conditions and the steps are the same but with a positive emphasis. The key is found in the biblical exhortation that, having "put off," we are now to "put on" (Col. 3:9, 10). The former exhortation refers primarily to the cleansing provided in the crucifixion and the latter to the enablement which is ours in the resurrection.

By a decision of faith we are to "put off," for example, the sin of selfishness and to "put on" the contrasting virtue of love. Or it may be lust, or doubt, or fear, or jealousy that must be rejected by faith and the virtues of purity, faith, courage, or praise that must be chosen in their place. The specific sin from which a believer may need cleansing and the specific virtue with which he may need enablement depends on his spiritual life and circumstances. The hypocrite, for example, needs a different type of enablement than the alcoholic.

79

We may not live as though the resurrection did not happen. It did happen and God has made adequate provision for our spiritual life. Therefore, we must make the spiritual decision to think and live in harmony with the resurrection (Rom. 6:11). We must also make the decision to live in the strength of the new nature (Rom. 6:12) and to do so in active dependence on God (Rom. 6:13).

These three conditions of success must be put into practice through the five steps mentioned earlier. We must sincerely and honestly acknowledge our need of help, confess our failure to manifest His grace, deliberately forsake our sins of omission, receive Jesus Christ as our specific enablement, and then live our daily lives practicing the virtues provided in Jesus Christ through the resurrection. These are all necessary decisions of faith.

Without this type of involvement with God and the resurrection, we may expect only failure.

The use of these five steps with regard to the crucifixion and the resurrection is one of emphasis only. In fact, the "putting off" and the "putting on" can be done at the same time. Once the believer learns how to make the decisions of faith, the rejection of selfishness and the appropriation of love may be but two aspects of the same decision.

The important factor is that the decisions be made as a response of genuine surrender and faith in God. Simply stating the words is worse than worthless. Mere platitudes invoke the judgment of God. (See Diagram 12).

GOD'S PROVISION: the new nature is a daily reality through the resurrection of Jesus Christ.

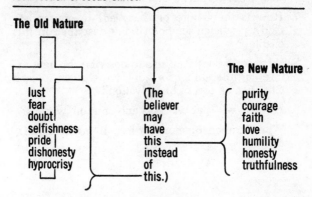

The Old Nature

The New Nature

lust	(The	purity
fear	believer	courage
doubt	may	faith
selfishness	have this —	love
pride	instead	humility
dishonesty	of	honesty
hyprocrisy	this.)	truthfulness

Diagram 12. *The key to success:* Daily choose by faith to live in the enablement of the new nature. We may have purity instead of lust, courage instead of fear, etc., through the crucifixion and resurrection of Jesus Christ.

Questions for Discussion

1. What does the Bible teach about those who do not keep Christ's commandments?

2. Which of the following—sinless perfection, continuing obedience, unbroken victory, deep introspection—is a basic characteristic of practical and progressive sanctification?

3. Explain why sanctification is a positive way of life.

4. What place does separation have in our sanctification?

5. Why must a Christian be especially watchful *after* he has learned to abstain from places, practices, and pleasures which hinder his growth in the Christian life?

81

6. The concept of being "alive unto God" is linked with what period of Christ's life?

7. How is the failure of Christians to appropriate God's provision for holy living described in this chapter?

8. What term does Paul use to describe the new nature and the ability for holy living given to each Christian as part of his salvation?

9. How do we "put off" sins and "put on" virtues?

10. Where can enablement for holy living be found?

The Ascension in the Believer's Daily Life

The ascension: Satan and the need of deliverance.

Standing between the Christian and a successful Christian life is not only his sinful pattern of life with its enmity against God, but also his implacable foe—Satan.

The Christian has an enemy. To deny his existence, to underrate his power, and to be ignorant of his methods, or to fail to give heed to the biblical warnings concerning Satan, can only result in spiritual loss.

The activity of Satan and his cunning counterfeits are disclosed in the Scriptures. He often comes as an "angel of light," in religious garb, to work with impunity among the children of God (II Cor. 11:13-15). So skilled is he in subterfuge and forgery that his activity is rarely recognized as evil. His influence is described as a "snare" (II Tim. 2:26).

In a piercing exposé of the character and the work of Satan, the Bible lists a number of descriptive titles, identifies him as a fallen angel of great ability, and illustrates what he does in his endeavor to strike out against God.

Satan is described as the believer's enemy through the title "adversary" (I Peter 5:8). This characterization of our foe is not to be taken lightly. Although it is true that the Christian belongs to God and is under His sovereign protection (Job 1:10), this does not mean the believer is automatically free from all satanic influences. By a misunderstanding of spiritual truths or through disobedience to God, a believer may permit such satanic intervention in his life that he will suffer great spiritual anxiety and loss. Look at what happened to Ananias and Sapphira (Acts 5:1-10).

As an adversary, Satan has a clear-cut goal. He will endeavor in every way possible to keep the believer from any type of spiritual progress, enjoyment, or usefulness. If we cannot be enslaved through physical sins (Luke 4:33), the adversary too often succeeds by leading us to overemphasize some spiritual truth or practice until it becomes a sin (Acts 5:1-11; II Cor. 2:10, 11; 11:13-15; I Tim. 3:6, 7). Every earnest Christian stands in great danger of such a spiritual perversion. This demonic activity is more prevalent in our churches today than we could imagine. As an angel of light, his ministry is almost beyond detection. Who would question the motivation of the legalist, the ascetic, the mystic, or the one caught up in unusual spiritual experiences? It would be plainly "unspiritual" to do so!

Our adversary works in the lives of Christians through temptation (I Thess. 3:5). We have been frankly told that we will not be tempted by God (James 1:13). Although one is often tempted through his own flesh (James 1:14), these activities may also find their source in the devil. Who does not face a constant barrage?

The activity of Satan is also described as a work of hindrance (I Thess. 2:18). How often the serious Christian has experienced this influence in his life! It must be recognized that the paramount goal of our adversary is to thwart and inhibit the believer's spiritual progress. The genuine Christian will have hindrances placed in his path by Satan. This was true of the apostle Paul as the above text indicates.

A third activity used by our adversary is that of deception (Rev. 12:9). With a heart that is deceitful (Jer. 17:9), the Christian is unusually vulnerable to this type of attack. In particular, Satan will endeavor to lead the believer into deception concerning spiritual truths and his own spiritual condition. The people of Judah, for example, were slowly led to believe that they were spiritual when they were not. Instead of loving God, they loved only religion. They were deceived. It was their religious deceit which finally brought their judgment and the Babylonian captivity (Jer. 7:1-16; 17:1-10). There are some things for which there is no cure—religiosity is one of these (Jer. 2:22; 8:5; 9:6; 11:11, 14; 14:12).

The believer may not allow his own religious feelings or conscience to be his authority. If he does, he is opening the door to Satan. How *we* feel about our spiritual condition is never authoritative; all authority resides in God and is made known through His work in history and His Word. When we confuse the voice of God with our own voice, we open ourselves to demonic deception (Gal. 6:3; II Tim. 3:13; James 1:22, 26; II Peter 2:13).

Satan is also given the title of "accuser" (Rev. 12:10). This designation characterizes one of the most serious and successful activities of our enemy. The Christian is not only accused before God (Job 1:9; Zech. 3:1), he is led, by Satan, into a state of false self-condemnation.

To accomplish this insidious work the devil adopts his "angel of light" subterfuge, and counterfeits the convicting work of the Holy Spirit. A serious Christian is suddenly engulfed by an intense awareness of personal guilt. He is made to feel, by Satan, as though he has sinned and is, therefore, out of fellowship with God and under His condemnation.

Under such a demonic attack the Christian is soon rendered helpless. No amount of confession relieves the "conviction" of sin or the sense of estrangement. His joy disappears, he is thwarted in his attempt to do Christian service and, most serious of all, he is confused when his confession of sin does not result in forgiveness and restored fellowship.

In this situation the Christian who has discernment of the ways of the enemy will take spiritual stock. He will recognize the ambiguity and confusion which has characterized his "conviction." This will indicate to him that he has not been the recipient of the ministry of the Holy Spirit but has been under the accusation of the devil.

When the Holy Spirit convicts of sin, His ministry is always characterized by clarity. The erring Christian is clearly shown what he has done wrong and what he is to do about it.

In direct contrast, the accusing work of Satan is always one of ambiguity. The Christian never knows what he has done or what he is to do to correct his situation. He is simply made to feel guilty and uneasy.

It is extremely important for the believer to learn this distinction between the ministry of the Holy Spirit and the counterfeiting of the devil. As long as the believer accepts the accusations of Satan as true, his condition is hopeless. He must recognize what has happened, resist the devil, and totally reject the accusations by a forthright decision of faith, such as: "In the name of the Lord Jesus Christ I reject that accusation and false quiet."

The titles of "murderer" and "liar" are also attributed to Satan (John 8:44). His objectives and actions in these areas are self-evident. His endeavors to take life and to pervert truth began in the Garden of Eden (I Tim. 2:14; I John 3:12) and will continue until the final judgment (I Tim. 4:1). We may not accept the demonic suggestion that our daily lives are without meaning and that self-destruction is the only "spiritual" alternative left. Nor may the believer allow himself to become the tool of Satan by accepting and repeating the insinuations and distortions of gossip. The apostle Paul flatly stated that the person who is a gossip has been influenced by Satan (I Tim. 5:13-15). It is important to recognize that of the seven things which God hates, the one who gossips has involved himself in six of these sins (Prov. 6:16-19)!

The believer has an enemy and is in desperate need of deliverance.

The ascension: Satan and the provision of deliverance.

The Lord Jesus Christ came into the world as man's representative to deliver His people from all demonic influence and to defeat Satan. As the last Adam He triumphed victoriously in the very area where the first Adam had completely failed (Rom. 5:12-19).

Under satanic temptation, the incarnate Lord Jesus Christ not only corrected the demonic half-truths which were suggested to Him but also repulsed the enemy and commanded him to leave His presence (Matt. 4:1-11). It is important to understand that Jesus Christ took refuge in and employed the written Word of God.

In His daily ministry Christ's power over Satan was continually manifested. There was a constant recognition, on the part of demons, of Christ's divine sonship, and of their total subjection to Him (Mark 3:11; 5:7; Luke 4:33-36).

The apostle John boldly stated that the reason Jesus Christ came into the world was to destroy the works of Satan (I John 3:8). The writer of Hebrews made a similar statement. He explained how the incarnation was necessary so that through His death, Christ could strip the devil of his power (Heb. 2:14) and deliver His people from Satan's bondage (Heb. 2:15).

The apostle Paul affirmed the atonement of Jesus Christ to be a public exposé of the defeat of Satan in which the Son of God triumphed gloriously (Col. 2:15). Because of this victory over Satan it must be recognized that although the Christian has an insidious and implacable foe in the devil, Satan is a defeated foe!

That which the Lord Jesus Christ obtained by His death He assumed and demonstrated in His ascension. The ascension, therefore, is filled with meaning for the believer. Christ has entered heaven, not only as intercessor (Heb. 4:14; 6:20; 7:25; 8:1; 9:11, 12) and the Head of the church (Eph. 1:22), to give gifts to His church (Eph. 4:8-11) and to bestow the Holy Spirit upon all believers (Acts 2:33), but also to rule over His enemies.

Jesus Christ was seated at the right hand of God in victory over Satan and all his forces of evil (Eph. 1:19-23; 2:5, 6; Heb. 1:13; I Peter 3:22). They were all placed "under His [Jesus'] feet."

This deliverance and position of authority over Satan has been legally given to the believer. We have been made to "sit together in heavenly places in Christ Jesus" (Eph. 2:6). Jesus Christ acted on our behalf as our representative. As a "joint-heir" with Christ we share in His victory (Rom. 8:17; Eph. 6:16).

The ascension: Satan and the provisions of deliverance.

In his salvation, the believer was delivered from the kingdom and power of Satan and brought into the kingdom of God (Acts 26:18; Col. 1:13). He, therefore, no longer lives under the dominion of the god of this world (Eph. 2:1-3; II Cor. 4:4). He has been set free.

However, it is one thing to be free from Satan in the area of salvation and quite another to maintain that freedom in the area of sanctification. The believer, through divine grace in salvation, now belongs to Jesus Christ. Therefore, he will never again belong to Satan. This does not mean, however, that Satan cannot make the believer's life miserable and ineffectual.

The Christian has been exhorted to resist the devil (James 4:7; I Peter 5:8, 9). This simply means to refuse to accept, or act in harmony with, the insinuations, accusations, or temptations of the enemy. The apostle Peter was right in warning us that this takes sobriety, vigilance, and steadfastness (I Peter 5:8, 9).

Except for unusual situations, the only way Satan can influence the Christian is through some aspect of ignorance or sinfulness. This is what the apostle Paul was referring to when he warned the Ephesian Christians, "Neither give place to the devil" (Eph. 4:27). When the believer allows the devil a "place" or "foothold" in his life, the devil will exploit that opportunity to the fullest.

There are at least four illustrations in the New Testament of giving opportunity to Satan. Two of

90

these illustrations have to do with the pastoral office and two with the membership in the church.

The apostle Paul warned Timothy that the pastor may not be a novice. A novice would be almost certain to become proud, and this would not only limit his fellowship with God, it would also open his life and ministry to the condemnation of the devil (I Tim. 3:6).

A second illustration regarding the church leader has to do with his testimony. He may not live in such a way that the non-Christian can accuse him of wrongdoing. He must be honest and consistent in daily life. If he is not, the devil will point it out and ruin him (I Tim. 3:7).

The third illustration has to do with forgiveness among church members. The church at Corinth had disciplined one of its members for immorality and was now exhorted to receive him back, since he had repented. Paul wrote to the church and warned them to forgive the man and to love him. Not to do so would have presented Satan an "advantage" (II Cor. 2:1-11).

Many Christians and churches have failed to obey this exhortation. Not only have the people displayed a lack of forgiveness but they have also added the sin of gossip. To make the situation worse, many repentant believers have not found love upon returning to their church but, instead, a cold stony indifference. Satan had been given the "advantage."

The fourth illustration describes two church members. Ananias and Sapphira pretended to be more spiritual than they were. Their profession did not match their inner walk with God. They had accepted a suggestion of Satan and had put it into practice. Their judgment serves as a warning to all hypocrites (Acts 5:1-11).

Any failure to obey God opens the door to satanic influence. When the Christian chooses to disobey God, he is acting as Eve did in the Garden. Eve allowed Satan to question the authority of God's Word and accepted the demonic interpretation. Having done this, it was quite easy for her to put the insinuations into practice. When the believer chooses to sin, he is acting, as Eve did, on the premise that the Word of God is not final authority. By failing to obey God we not only destroy our spirituality, but we also allow Satan to ensnare us (II Tim. 2:25, 26).

To escape this tragic situation and its inexorable result we must learn to obey God and resist the devil. In response to satanic questioning of the Word of God and deceptive insinuations concerning the will of God, we must steadfastly affirm the truthfulness of the Word and will of God (I Peter 5:8, 9; Matt. 4:1-11).

In obeying the exhortation to resist the devil, the apostle Paul stated that the most important factor was understanding and using the "shield of faith" (Eph. 6:16). This we are to do "above all." The shield is more valuable than any of the other items of the Christian's armor (Eph. 6:11-18). This "shield" is a symbolic representation of Christ's victory and the believer's decision of faith. To understand this will successfully thwart the attacks of Satan. The apostle Peter stated the same truth (I Peter 5:9).

The faith to which both Peter and Paul were referring is the believer's wholehearted trust in

and commitment to Jesus Christ and His successful triumph over Satan. This faith is the decision
to stand in the value of and to appropriate the
power of Christ's victory. The Christian has every
right to do this since the power of Christ's work
has been imputed to him. When we make the decision to obey God fully, to trust in the person and
work of Jesus Christ, and to live accordingly, we
will learn what it means to resist the devil, and
we will have the ability to do so. We will have a
"shield of faith."

These exhortations are summarized in the Book
of Revelation in the description of the overcomers
(Rev. 12:11). The secret of their victory over Satan
was threefold. The reference to "the blood of the
Lamb" indicates the victorious triumph of Jesus
Christ in whom they trusted. "The word of their
testimony" refers to their decisions of faith to appropriate Christ's victory. And, finally, the statement, "they loved not their lives unto the death"
portrays their committal to Jesus Christ even
though it meant death.

The believer must learn to pray aggressively
and wear the armor provided by God. A sample
of such a prayer is found in the Appendix. Use
this prayer for a few days until you learn to pray
this way.

For too many Christians this description of life
is entirely foreign to their daily existence. The
problem is not with the provision of God nor with
the biblical exhortations. The reason many Christians do not experience deliverance or even feel
the need of divine help is because of their attitude: they couldn't care less! With that kind of
attitude about spiritual things the average Chris-

93

tian will very likely not be bothered by satanic influences. He has made his own life ineffectual! (See Diagram 13.)

GOD'S PROVISION: legal and practical deliverance from Satan through the crucifixion, resurrection, and ascension of Jesus Christ our Lord.

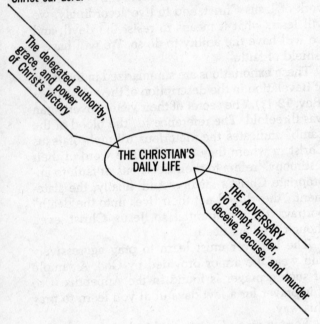

The delegated authority, grace, and power of Christ's victory

THE CHRISTIAN'S DAILY LIFE

THE ADVERSARY
To tempt, hinder, deceive, accuse, and murder

Diagram 13. *The key to success:* Resist the devil by rejecting his insinuations and temptations. Refuse, in the name of the Lord Jesus Christ, all his attempts to enter your daily life. If the adversary gains entrance through sin, repent, apologize to God, and take back the ground you have given to the devil. Maintain the armor provided by God. Pray about this every day.

94

Questions for Discussion

1. In what guise does Satan seek to subvert the work of God in a *religious* way?

2. As the believer's adversary, what is Satan's goal?

3. Explain Satan's role as a deceiver.

4. What should a Christian do when Satan tries to oppress him with guilt?

5. What is Satan's tool for snaring the soul described in Proverbs 6:16-19?

6. What did Jesus do when He was tempted by Satan?

7. Which aspect of Christ's ascension applies with special significance to all believers?

8. How did James preface his injunction to believers to "resist the devil and he will flee from you"?

9. Name some ways a believer might give place to the devil.

10. What characterized the victorious believers mentioned in Revelation 12?

Chapter 9

Pentecost in the Believer's Daily Life

Pentecost: The promise of the Holy Spirit in the Old Testament.

Theologically speaking, everything that has been said up to this point is purely theory. Only with the ministry of the Holy Spirit may one legitimately speak of daily practice. God the Holy Spirit has come to apply the provision the Lord Jesus Christ has obtained for the believer. Through His work of the new birth, the Christian has been transformed; and through His work of anointing the believer is enabled to live the Christian life successfully.

One of the most encouraging and impressive promises of the Old Testament has to do with the Holy Spirit. It is found in Joel 2:28, 29. There God promises that the day will come when He will pour out His Spirit equally on all His people. In that day it will not make a difference if one is a man or a woman, old or young, master or servant. All will receive the Holy Spirit alike.

This does not mean that the Old Testament saints were without the ministry of the Holy Spirit. When Jesus Christ said to Nicodemus that a person must be born of the Spirit to enter the kingdom of God, His stipulation applied equally well to all people in all time (John 3:3, 5). It is evident that the Old Testament saints were recipients of the ministry of the Holy Spirit in the new birth, in that they are used as an illustration of salvation to New Testament saints. According to the writer of Hebrews, salvation by faith was true of Abel (Heb. 11:4), David (Rom. 4:6), Abraham (Rom. 4:10-25; Gal. 3:6-14), and Rahab (James 2:25, 26) are similar examples.

It must be recognized that there was also an anointing by the Holy Spirit of certain individuals in the Old Testament. Bezaleel and Aholiab were anointed to enable them to build the tabernacle (Exod. 35:30-35). Moses (Num. 11:25) and Joshua (Num. 27:18) were anointed to lead the children of Israel. The various judges were anointed to deliver the people of God from their enemies (Judges 3:10; 6:34, etc.). Saul (I Sam. 10:10) and David (I Sam. 16:13) were anointed as kings over Israel. The Holy Spirit came upon the prophets to inspire them to speak forth the message given to them by God (I Chron. 12:18; II Chron. 15:1; 20:14; 24:20). Even upon Balaam, a false prophet, God placed His Spirit so the demonic endeavors of Balak would be thwarted (Num. 24:2).

Pentecost: The promise of the Holy Spirit in the New Testament.

As great as this ministry was in Old Testament times, God promised through Joel that a day would come when it would be transcended. This theme was taken up by the last of the Old Testament prophets and further explained. John the Baptist stated that the Holy Spirit would be given by the Messiah (John 1:33). This clarifying statement is of great importance. It determines the theological perspective for all the New Testament statements concerning the Holy Spirit, specifically that the ministry of the Spirit would always be inseparably related to the person of the Lord Jesus and the carrying out of His purpose.

Additional clarification concerning the ministry of the Holy Spirit was given by the Lord Jesus Christ Himself. There are five passages in the New Testament in which the coming of the Holy Spirit is further clarified.

The first is in John 7:37-39. Jesus Christ stated that all those who are thirsty, and come to Him and drink, believing on Him, would themselves become the source of living water. The apostle John observed that this invitation and promise revolved around the coming of the Holy Spirit who had not yet been given.

In this passage there are two factors of importance which have been pointed out previously. The first has to do with how one receives the Holy Spirit. This, we are told, is by believing on the Lord Jesus Christ. The second has to do with the result of His ministry in our lives. We will become the means of life-giving help to other people. These words of the Lord Jesus boldly cut through the worry and uncertainty so characteristic of many Christians. Here is the answer to the doubt and uncertainty which revolve around the question of personal ability to live a meaningful life.

What is His answer to our weakness in life and service? He states that we must thirst for Him, come to Him, and drink of Him in faith. As always, the problem is not in the provision, but in our lack of appropriation. When we learn how to respond by faith and thereby give Jesus Christ His rightful place, there will be a spontaneous ministry of the Holy Spirit to us and through us. Faith and love must be more than verbal pronouncements; they must be activities of life. That which determines our relationship to the Holy Spirit is our relationship to Jesus Christ.

The second passage of clarification is found in John 14:16-20. Here the Lord Jesus characterizes the person and work of the Holy Spirit by ascribing two titles to Him. The first is "Comforter" which means in the original language, "One called alongside." By this title we are taught that the Holy Spirit will be a constant help to the believer, as one called to his aid, by standing alongside. It is significant that the Lord Jesus also stated that the Holy Spirit would be "another Comforter." He was, therefore, to take the place of Christ Himself with His disciples. The significance of this truth is almost beyond human comprehension. That God Himself, the Holy Spirit, would come to us to be our Helper is overwhelming!

Another title of the Holy Spirit is that of "Spirit of truth." This indicates the purpose of His coming. He is the divine Teacher of truth. Because non-Christians reject the truth and love darkness rather than light (John 3:19), they cannot receive nor will they receive this ministry of the Spirit. However, the Holy Spirit has come to every believer to be his Teacher (I John 2:20, 27).

Using these two titles, the Lord Jesus explained how He would come to the disciples in the coming of the Holy Spirit (John 14:18); and how they would become the recipients of assurance and illumination (John 14:19, 20). The same promise is summarized later in the chapter (John 14:25, 26).

A third passage of instruction in this farewell discourse is found in John 15:26, 27. The titles of the Holy Spirit are restated as well as the emphasis on the relationship of His ministry to that of the Lord Jesus and to God the Father. The additional element here is the focus on the purpose of His coming. The Lord Jesus said, "he shall testify of me: And ye also shall bear witness. ..." The Holy Spirit will comfort, instruct, and illuminate those who believe on the Lord Jesus so that they will be enabled, through His indwelling presence, to bear witness themselves.

The fourth reference to the ministry of the Holy Spirit is found in John 16:7-16. Here we are told that the Holy Spirit will convict the non-Christian of sin, righteousness, and of a future judgment. All mankind are the recipients of this reproof.

In addition to what has been said in the previous passages about the work of the Holy Spirit in the believer, this passage includes two further statements of great importance. The first is found in verse 13, ". . . he shall not speak of himself. . . ." This means that the Holy Spirit will not draw attention to Himself. This profound statement, expressed so simply, indicates that the entire ministry of the Spirit is away from Himself. All endeavors, whether by the individual Christian or by a church or denomination, to place the Holy Spirit at the center of attention and instruction is, therefore, under divine censure.

The second statement clearly expresses the purpose of the Holy Spirit's ministry. It is found in verse 14. The Lord Jesus said, "He shall glorify me. . . ." Instead of drawing attention to Himself, the Holy Spirit would magnify Jesus Christ. This is His goal in the life of the individual believer and in the ministry of the church. Jesus Christ is to be given His rightful place at the center of all things. When the believer or church chooses to do this, then there is a cooperation with the Holy Spirit and the result can only be spiritual success. When this is not done, weakness will inevitably follow. The importance of these truths can hardly be overemphasized.

The fifth passage of explanation is found in Acts 1:4, 5, 8. The Lord Jesus, after His resurrection from the grave, instructed His followers to wait in Jerusalem for the fulfilment of the promises concerning the Holy Spirit. They were to be baptized with the Spirit and would thereby receive the power or ability to be witnesses for Jesus Christ throughout the whole world.

Pentecost: The manifestation of the Holy Spirit.

Fifty days after the crucifixion of the Lord Jesus, the Old Testament and New Testament promises regarding the coming of the Holy Spirit were fulfilled. In obedience to the instruction of the Lord Jesus (Acts 1:4, 5, 8), a group of His disciples were praying together when the Holy Spirit descended on them. With the sound of a great wind and with the appearance of fire, the Holy Spirit filled all the disciples (Acts 2:1-4).

As a further demonstration of the presence of the Holy Spirit, all the disciples began to speak with tongues so that the many strangers in Jerusalem heard the gospel preached in their own language. As a result three thousand persons responded to the commands and promise of the gospel and were baptized (Acts 2:4-11, 37-47).

The apostle Peter that same day explained the meaning of this great event. He quoted the promise concerning the Holy Spirit as given in Joel 2:28, 29 and indicated that it had now been fulfilled (Acts 2:14ff). The coming of the Holy Spirit, Peter expounded, was due to the activity of the ascended Lord Jesus who had poured out the Spirit on His people (Acts 2:33). Pentecost, therefore, was further and conclusive evidence of the resurrection and exaltation of the Lord Jesus Christ as the Son of God (Acts 2:29-36).

It is important to understand that Pentecost, like the crucifixion, resurrection, and ascension, happened only once. It is also important to see that the church, now called the body of Christ (Eph.

1:22, 23), was brought into existence at this out-pouring of the Holy Spirit. Before this time the church is spoken of as yet in the future (Matt. 16:18). But now on the day of Pentecost the church is described as present (Acts 2:47), and continually referred to from this time on.

The spiritual value of these two truths is of great significance to the believer. Today when an individual repents of sin and receives Jesus Christ as Savior and Lord, he is baptized by the Holy Spirit into the church (I Cor. 12:13). By this great act, the believer becomes a member of the church and receives all the benefits of the day of Pentecost.

The Holy Spirit has come! The promises have been fulfilled. The body of Christ has been brought into existence and is made up of people baptized with the Holy Spirit. To become a Christian means one is added to that baptized group and in turn receives all the spiritual benefits the first disciples received on the day of Pentecost (I Cor. 12:13-27).

In order to avoid confusion, it is necessary to distinguish between the spiritual benefits of Pentecost and the public demonstration of that day. The public display of power in the wind, the fire, and the speaking with tongues was given by God to indicate the importance and significance of that great event. The wind and fire would immediately call to mind the supernatural activity of God with the prophets (I Kings 18:38; 19:11, 12; Ezek. 1:4; etc.), and the speaking in tongues was a public evidence that the promise of Joel concerning an anointing of *all* of God's people had indeed come to pass. Such a manifestation of power also char-acterized the crucifixion, resurrection, and ascension. The Christian now possesses the legal benefits of all of these great deeds of God. It would be as wrong for one to expect the wind, fire, and tongues of the day of Pentecost to characterize his relationship with God today as to expect the darkness of the crucifixion, the earthquake of the resurrection, or the appearance of angels of the ascension.

What are the benefits of the day of Pentecost which all believers now possess? Scripture describes this great provision of God under five headings. The first we have already considered, that of baptism with the Holy Spirit whereby one is brought into a saving relationship with the Lord Jesus Christ and made a member of the church which is His body (I Cor. 12:13). When does this happen? This important event happens the moment one believes on Jesus Christ as Savior and Lord. In fact, all five benefits come to pass at exactly the same time.

The second benefit of the day of Pentecost is described as the new birth (John 3:3, 5). In this act of the Holy Spirit the repentant and believing sinner is given the spiritual life obtained from him by Jesus Christ in His atonement (John 10:10; I John 5:9-13).

The third benefit is that of being indwelt by the Holy Spirit. The believer thereby becomes the temple of the Holy Spirit (I Cor. 3:16, 17; 6:10; II Cor. 6:16).

The fourth benefit is described as being sealed with the Holy Spirit (II Cor. 1:22; Eph. 1:13, 14; 4:30). The term *seal* is taken from the practice of "sealing" a legal document with a bit of wax into which an official seal or stamp was pressed. The emphasis here is on the truth of ownership. The believer, by this act of the Holy Spirit, is shown to belong to God. This work of the Holy Spirit is further described as the "earnest" or pledge that all the future benefits of redemption will also be given the believer (II Cor. 1:22; 5:5; Eph. 1:14).

The fifth benefit is the bestowal of gifts by the Holy Spirit. Every Christian has been given some ability or talent so that he can make a meaningful contribution to the furtherance of God's plan. It is important to see that the apostle Paul used the analogy of the human body to describe the church. As every member of the body must contribute to the full expression of the person, so every member of the church has been given a gift and this gift must be utilized so that the church may express itself fully (I Cor. 12:4-31; Eph. 4:7-16). This is God's provision not only for the individual believer but also for the furtherance of the local church. When God's people are spiritually alert and exercising their divine gifts, the individual church will find itself adequately staffed with workers.

These five benefits appear to be subsumed in the Scripture under the term *anointing* (II Cor. 1:21; I John 2:20, 27). The Christian is, therefore, spoken of as one who has been anointed by the Holy Spirit. This again points back to the ministry of the Holy Spirit in the Old Testament. The New Testament emphasis is also indicated in that all the believers now receive this anointing alike. And all have received the five great benefits of Pentecost.

But now we must face a practical question of spiritual importance. If all believers possess these benefits of Pentecost, why are these benefits not more enjoyed and utilized? What a tremendous thing it is to be baptized, born again, indwelt, sealed, and gifted by the Holy Spirit! How dare we be filled with uncertainty and weakness!

The answer is clear and yet hard to confess. The fact of these great benefits depends on the work of God within us. The resultant assurance, power, and enjoyment of these benefits depends on us. It is one thing to possess this provision of Pentecost and quite another to know how to live, and then to so live that this divine provision may be adequately manifested in our daily lives.

Pentecost: The manifestation of the Holy Spirit.

We have been commanded by God to "be filled with the Spirit" (Eph. 5:18). The Christian has no vote in this matter. Living a Spirit-filled life is not optional. And to choose to disobey God condemns one to a life largely devoid of divine fellowship, grace, love, and purpose.

What does it mean to be filled with the Holy Spirit? It means, in all simplicity, to be surrendered to God (Rom. 12:1, 2) so that the Holy Spirit can do in and through us what He was sent to do. Endless numbers of books have been written explaining this one profound truth. Have so many words confused us?

The Christian is seriously warned against hindering this ministry of the Holy Spirit in his life.

Ananias and Sapphira are held up as an example of lying to (deceiving) or tempting the Holy Spirit (Acts 5:3, 9). Stephen accused those who refused the truth of the Word of God of resisting the Holy Spirit (Acts 7:51). The apostle Paul stated that the believer who is unconcerned and slothful about putting the Word of God into daily practice is grieving the Holy Spirit (Eph. 4:30). And those Christians who scorn and deride the expression of the Holy Spirit in their own lives and the lives of others are quenching the Holy Spirit (I Thess. 5:19).

These four sins clearly and tragically describe what it means to practice a lack of surrender to God. They vividly indicate the anti-surrender which characterizes the lives of most Christians. How easy it is to practice these four sins by substituting pretense for honesty, doubt for faith, disobedience for obedience, and an attitude of scornful self-complacency for one of grateful desire for every manifestation of the Holy Spirit.

And now we know why we are not Spirit filled! We lie to, resist, grieve, and quench the Holy Spirit! The lethargic unconcern manifested by many Christians about this indisputable truth proves the correctness of this accusation.

What must we do to live a genuine Christian life and be filled with the Spirit? First of all, we must stop blaming God for our being spiritually empty (Jer. 2:5, 13). In a close connection with this, we must stop contriving theological reasons for our lack and thereby turn our faults into virtues! God is not to blame. The Holy Spirit has come—there is no need to wait for Him. Ever

107

since the day of Pentecost, which happened only once, every believer has had all the value and provision of Pentecost given to him in his salvation (Rom. 8:9). We are at fault.

Secondly, we must confess our sins and stop committing them. We must stop pretending—stop acting as though we hadn't sinned, acting as though we are right with God. We must stop resisting the Holy Spirit—stop being so irresponsible about truth and our personal progress with God. We must stop grieving the Holy Spirit—stop being so unconcerned about putting the Word of God into practice. We must stop quenching the Holy Spirit—stop scoffing at those who are our examples in spirituality and start thirsting for God ourselves.

Thirdly, we must thoroughly understand why the Holy Spirit indwells us and learn how to cooperate with Him. He was sent to achieve clearly defined goals in our lives. These goals we must make our own by deliberate decisions of faith and practice.

The first goal the Holy Spirit has been commissioned to fulfill is that of glorifying Jesus Christ in the believer. Before the Christian can practice honesty he must choose to become a holy person. Before he can practice love, joy, peace, etc., (the fruit of the Spirit, Gal. 5:22, 23), he must experience love, joy, peace. The Holy Spirit has been sent to take the work of Jesus Christ in His crucifixion, resurrection, and ascension and make personal application of this cleansing, enablement, and deliverance in the very character of the believer. This is what sanctification is all about.

This is how the Holy Spirit leads and teaches the believer to mortify (put to death) the sinful attitudes and practices of the flesh (Rom. 8:1-13) and to experience the freedom of sonship (Rom. 8:14-17).

We are, therefore, to "Walk [live] in the Spirit" (Gal. 5:16). When this is done there will be a freedom, a deliverance from the overpowering desires of the law of sin (Gal. 5:16). Without this cooperation, a deadening, discouraging tension is set up in our lives (Gal. 5:17) and we live without a sense of purpose and progress and without love and joy and peace.

The Holy Spirit has thus been sent to enable us to give Jesus Christ His rightful place at the center of our lives. We must learn how to give Him that place as our Lord, our sanctification, as the Head of the church, as the Lord of the harvest field, and as the living Word.

How tragically different is the biblical description of the Spirit-filled life from what we often see in our own lives! Many Christians have earnestly tried to practice the Christian life without realizing that the real need was within. As a result the practice was partially a pretense and the vicious cycle started again.

The second goal the Holy Spirit has been sent to achieve is that of glorifying the Lord Jesus Christ through the believer (John 15:26, 27). The emphasis here is on daily practice and witnessing. The Lord Jesus often spoke of this as a spontaneous result of the indwelling Holy Spirit (John 7:37-39; 15:26, 27; Acts 1:8). When the believer cooperates with the Holy Spirit in regard to the

GOD'S PROVISION: the enablement of a daily anointing through the ministry of the Holy Spirit.

The Christian has been   anointed
baptized
born again
indwelt
sealed
gifted

and may have	love	instead of	selfishness
	joy	" "	despair
	peace	" "	anxiety
	longsuffering	" "	impatience
	gentleness	" "	rudeness
	goodness	" "	malice
	faithfulness	" "	insincerity
	meekness	" "	dogmatism
	self-control	" "	instability

He has been given a divine enablement for
the enjoyment of spiritual things (Rom. 14:17)
an understanding of salvation (Rom. 8:15-17)
an understanding of Scripture (John 16:12-15)
daily strength and holiness (Rom. 8:13, 14)
a successful prayer life (Rom. 8:26)
witnessing (Acts 1:8)
guidance (John 16:13)

Diagram 14. *The key to success:* The believer must learn to co-operate actively with the ministry of the indwelling Holy Spirit (Eph. 4:30).

first goal of personal sanctification, this second goal will be achieved automatically. The believer will then be, in character, a witness, and he will not find it difficult to speak up for his Lord. This is a self-condemning explanation of our lack of faithful witnessing.

What determines our daily relationship to the Holy Spirit? What does it mean, and how are we to be filled? We must be taken up with the Lord Jesus Christ! We must respond to Him and His Word by faith and love and thereby give Him His rightful place in our lives. We must learn to live in fellowship with God and in daily obedience. The Holy Spirit has been sent to glorify Jesus Christ in our lives, and when we give Him His rightful place, then we are filled with the Holy Spirit. This is why the Holy Spirit is called, "the Spirit of Christ" (Rom. 8:9). (See Diagram 14.)

Questions for Discussion

1. How were the Old Testament people saved?
2. What role did the Holy Spirit play in the Old Testament?
3. How do we receive the Holy Spirit?
4. Explain why the Holy Spirit is called "the Comforter."
5. What Scripture text tells us that the Spirit's great work is to "glorify" the Lord Jesus?
6. What is the baptism of the Holy Spirit and what does it do for the believer?
7. What is the seal of the Spirit and what does it do?
8. What does it mean to be "filled" with the Spirit?
9. What must we do in order to be filled with the Spirit?
10. How can a believer know as a daily living reality in his life the cleansing, enablement, and deliverance wrought for him by the Lord Jesus in His crucifixion, resurrection, and ascension?

Chapter 10

"And now faith is . . ."

The biblical demand: Only faith will do!

It is one thing to know the truth but it is quite another to put the truth into practice. The desire to be a successful Christian is not enough. Nor is it sufficient to give an intellectual assent to Scripture. The biblical demand is quite clear—only faith will do! ". . . without faith it is impossible to please him . . ." (Heb. 11:6).

Therefore, the issue is not this or that sin; it is not our money, nor our talent, nor our time, nor our work, nor is it even the various doctrines we accept. The issue is not our prayer life and its length; it is not our service for Christ and its amount; it is not our church attendance and its frequency; it is not our Bible study and its depth; it is not our sincerity and its transparency—the issue is faith.

What is this necessary ingredient which acts as a catalyst between knowledge and practice? What is it that God demands of us?

Faith will never be understood as long as it is considered to be, and investigated as, an abstract idea or an isolated virtue. Faith is inseparably related to genuine Christianity. While the term may be used in a great variety of ways, such as putting one's faith in a person, an instrument, or a medicine, in the biblical sense faith is much more strictly defined. It is not enough to say that the person who believes in a false religion has faith. Of course he has faith, but it is condemned by the Bible as false. The biblical Christian and the Buddhist both have faith, but the faith of the former is true and the faith of the latter is spurious, even though his sincerity may be beyond reproach.

Biblical Christianity revolves around the person of Jesus Christ. Therefore, biblical faith is inseparably related to correct belief and action regarding Jesus Christ.

Biblical Christianity is rooted in the redemptive work of Jesus Christ in history. Therefore, biblical faith is inseparably related to correct belief and action regarding the atonement.

Biblical Christianity is based on the revelation of God in the Scriptures. Therefore, biblical faith is inseparably related to correct belief and action regarding the Bible.

Perhaps at this point it would be helpful to ask about a definition of biblical faith. While there are many facets to faith, a definition would include at least the following points:

113

Faith is the response of the total person to God as a person in loving submission, trust, and obedience; in and through the person of Jesus Christ as the Revelation of God and Redeemer of mankind, who as the sovereign Lord offers Himself to the believer, through the ministry of the Holy Spirit and the Scriptures, as his daily sufficiency.

The biblical explanation (1): Faith is a decision to respond correctly to God.

Faith is not a feeling but a decision. This is what is meant by the word *response* in the above definition. Faith is, therefore, a correct response to God. Unbelief and doubt are the opposite of faith. They are incorrect responses to God.

God has revealed Himself. What we choose to do with Him and His Word is very important. When we make a choice to obey the commandments of God and to claim His promises, we have made a decision. It is a correct response to the God of the Word. It is faith. When we choose to disobey God through His commandments and to reject His promises, we have also made a decision, but it is an incorrect response—doubt and unbelief—to the God of the Word.

In Hebrews 11 we are given a series of illustrations of faith. A number of individuals are described in many circumstances of life, all making a decision to respond harmoniously to God and His Word. Moses is a good example of such decision-making. In verses 24-28 there are five words which illustrate his response to God. These words are "refused," "choosing," "esteeming," "for-

114

sook," and "kept." Each indicates a decision on the part of Moses. God had revealed His will to Moses: he was not to stay in Egypt; he was to lead the Israelites into Canaan. These five words indicate how he responded to God by making the right decisions to obey God's Word. This is what the Bible means by faith.

How the Christian feels about his faith and ability to live by faith has nothing to do with it. The all-important factor is his choice and decision.

Faith has three very clear characteristics. The first is that of submission to God and His Word. Without this necessary ingredient it is ridiculous for us to think we can make a correct decision of faith. Any lack of concern for the will of God and all decisions to disobey the Word of God not only bring a disruption of fellowship in the life of the Christian but also make a decision of faith in the area of his insubordination impossible.

The second characteristic of faith is the practice of obedience. Genuine faith is a correct response to God and this is always inseparable from obedience in daily life. This is one reason why it is so difficult for us to live by faith when we do not wish to obey God. It is absurd for us to try to exercise faith about a matter when we are apathetic about obeying God or when we have made the decision not to obey! This is part of the theme of Hebrews 11. Each illustration of faith in that chapter is also an illustration of obedience. Faith is not primarily a sense of dependency on God. It is a decision to submit to God through His Word and to put the Word of God into daily practice.

The third characteristic of faith is that of trust. This is also a necessary ingredient for biblical faith. It is the inseparable companion to submission and the practice of obedience. When Moses made the decision to submit to the directive of God to lead the Israelites out of Egypt, and sought to obey God, he did so in trust. He trusted God to give him wisdom and strength to obey and also trusted God to make the journey possible. At the very least, this trust involved making the Israelites willing to go, dealing with Pharoah and his armies, opening the Red Sea, and supplying food and water.

God expects us to trust Him. When we choose to obey His Word, and put that choice into daily obedience, God pledges Himself to make His will possible. Abraham expressed this trust in the words, "And being fully persuaded that, what he had promised, he was able also to perform" (Rom. 4:21). This third characteristic of faith was also expressed by Paul. During the storm at sea he said, "Wherefore, sirs, be of good cheer: for I believe God, that it shall be even as it was told me" (Acts 27:25).

God is worthy of our trust. He is the truth. What He has promised He will fulfill and what He has commanded He will make possible.

The biblical explanation (2): Faith has a person as its object—God.

Biblical faith is not to be confused with personal self-confidence, nor is it trust in the goodness of man. We have not been told to put faith in

116

the church, nor in a group of religious ideas. We are to trust God.

Only God is the object of biblical faith. In the hour of the disciples' greatest need, the Lord Jesus simply asked them to trust Him (John 14:1). The message of the Bible is unmistakable on this point. "Abraham believed *God* ..." (Rom. 4:3). "Have faith in *God*" (Mark 11:22). It was the Lord Jesus who said, "And if I say the truth, why do ye not believe *me*?" (John 8:46, italics mine).

This simple truth can be an immeasurable help in the Christian life. Faith is not blind. It is not an ambiguous trust in some abstract entity. It is not a leap in the dark. God is the object of faith. Because of His revelation, God and His will can be known and acted on (John 17:3). There may be times when God will ask us to trust Him without the benefit of inner assurance or compatible circumstances. This, undoubtedly, was true of Job (Job 13:15) and Abraham (Rom. 4:16-21). But even this is not "blind faith." These men believed God and His Word, in spite of the adverse circumstances. They are presented to us as examples.

This truth of having God as the object of faith includes one of the most encouraging facets of the Christian life. It is a cure for that nagging question which constantly plagues the serious Christian regarding the amount and the strength of his faith. When we face a difficult situation we often ask, "I wonder if I have enough faith to cope with this?" or, "Is my faith strong enough to endure?"

The comforting factor in all of this is that such questions are irrelevant. The amount of faith is not the issue. When the Lord Jesus called the

117

faith of the woman of Canaan "great," He was referring to the clear-cut decisions she had made and the persistence with which she maintained them (Matt. 15:21-28). The issue is not how we feel about the amount of our faith; it is whether we will exercise faith! It is whether we will make the right decisions.

This is also true concerning the strength of faith. Since God is the object of faith, He is the source of faith's strength. The exhortation is, ". . . be strong in the Lord, and in the power of his might" (Eph. 6:10). When Paul said, "I can do all things through Christ which strengtheneth me" (Phil. 4:13), he was including his ability to believe God. Abraham was commended by God for having a "strong" faith (Rom. 4:19, 20). What is meant by this passage is that Abraham made the right decisions in regard to the revealed will of God and persisted in those decisions. The term *strong* is in contrast to the term *weak in faith* in verse 19. There Abraham is commended for not allowing adverse circumstances to hinder his response to the known will of God.

The strength of faith does not reside in the Christian. We may not use the excuse of weakness. When we state or imply, "I didn't have enough faith," or "My faith wasn't strong enough," we are simply blaming God for our failure or we are confessing our ignorance in understanding biblical faith. When we want to make the right decision of faith and desire to practice the accompanying will of God, we will receive all the strength we need from God!

118

The biblical explanation (3): Faith has a context—love.

In Galatians 5:6, the apostle Paul stated, "For in Jesus Christ neither circumcision availeth any thing, nor uncircumcision; but faith which worketh by love."

What does "avail" to bring the grace and power of God into our lives? By use of the term *circumcision* the apostle Paul indicated that all the legalism and ceremonialism of the Jewish Christians availed nothing. And by use of the word *uncircumcision* he specified the ecstatic emotional religious experiences of the Gentiles as also unavailing.

We must accept this frank evaluation. No amount of mere rule-keeping, Bible study, church attendance, Christian service, or emotional experience will "avail" in our lives unless it is a genuine expression of faith and love.

The issue is again shown to be faith. And here we are told that the context of faith, that which makes faith "work," is love. Without love, according to the apostle Paul, faith does not "work"; it is "inactive."

Now we understand that the correct response to God has two clearly discernible aspects. The two sides to this response are faith and love. Both are necessary; one does not exist without the other. These two are often united in the Bible (I Cor. 13:13; I Thess. 1:3; I Tim. 1:5)

What is this love which provides the necessary context for faith? It is love for God! To love God means to give Him His rightful place in our daily

119

life. It is to recognize Him for who He is and to live consistently in harmony with Him. This is the reason why love and obedience are always inseparably related in the Bible (John 14:15; I John 5:3).

The failure to love God genuinely is the most serious hindrance to faith in the life of all Christians. We cannot be unconcerned about the will of God and then expect to be able to claim the promises of God. Any and all failure to give God His rightful place strips us of the discernment and ability to make a decision of faith. Because of this truth, the words *repent* and *confess* are often coupled with the word *believe* in the Bible. Before we can believe, sin—the result of lack of love—must be dealt with.

Faith cannot exist as a daily experience without the reality of love as a daily experience. Faith and love are mutually dependent. This is the answer to the question of why faith is necessary to please God (Heb. 11:6) and yet love for God is the first commandment (Matt. 22:37).

When we choose to disobey God, by the sin of either commission or omission, we manifest our failure to love Him adequately. Such a choice will leave us without the ability to fellowship with God and to respond to Him by faith. The degree of loss is determined by the seriousness of the choice to disobey.

The biblical explanation (4):   Faith has a basis—Scripture.

Faith is a decision to respond correctly to God. The content of that decision and response is determined by Scripture. This is clearly seen in the eleventh chapter of Hebrews. The sacrifice which Abel offered had been specified by God as the only one acceptable. Abel's offering was a correct response to God's revelation. Noah built the ark in response to divine directives. Abraham left his homeland and traveled toward Palestine as a response to God's command. The Word of God was the basis of their faith.

In this way faith is rooted in the Scripture. We have been commanded to mix the Word of God with faith (Heb. 4:1-3). We fulfill the commandment by the persistent effort to put the Word of God into practice in all areas of life as an expression of our love for God.

Our failure to read, to study, and to understand Scripture will be a serious handicap in the expression of our faith and the obedience which should follow. How can we obey God when we do not know His commandments? How can we claim His promises when we do not know their content? How can we believe when we do not know what to believe? (Rom. 10:14). "So then faith cometh by hearing, and hearing by the word of God" (Rom. 10:17).

The first step, therefore, toward pleasing God in the expression of faith and love, is an inquiry into the Word of God. Since Scripture is the basis of our faith, it is necessarily the foundation of all of the other facets of our Christian life. Without an understanding of the Word and will of God, grace, peace, power, and progress are impossible.

The importance of this truth is paramount. No amount of pious effort can be substituted for a simple understanding of the Bible. All efforts to make progress in the Christian life will be thwarted until serious steps are consistently and persistently taken to become familiar with the basic message and themes of the Bible.

The biblical exhortation: The steps in a decision of faith.

Progress in the Christian life is usually a step-by-step process. This is particularly true in the area of sanctification. When we are led by the Holy Spirit to the recognition of some sin in our life, then it is important that we know what to do with that sin. One of the clearest statements in this regard is found in I John 1:9, "If we confess our sins, he is faithful and just to forgive us our sins, and to cleanse us from all unrighteousness." In order to mix this Word of God with faith (Heb. 4:1-3), we must obey God in a very personal and practical manner and put the verse into practice.

The first step is to *confess the sin*—as a sin! If we are not willing to do this, there is no need to start praying. No amount of weeping, lamenting, and making resolutions can take the place of a simple honest confession. When we have disobeyed God and acted out of harmony with His Word, we must in a very specific, pointed, sincere, thorough, and honest way confess our sin for what it really is. We must bluntly name ourselves and our sin. If we have sinned through gossip or doubt or laziness or immorality, we must confess it as such. "Lord, I confess to You that I am a gossip and I have used my tongue to hurt my friend," would be a good way to begin. This confession is a decision, an enactment of faith.

The second step is to *forsake the sin*. This is also a decision. It is the only correct decision which we can make following an acknowledgment of sin. There is no other alternative. This also must be a sincere and honest choice in the presence of God. Any pretense here will destroy all hope of divine help. We must take a stand against our sin and then deliberately and consistently carry out our decision. When Augustine was thirty-two years old, he suddenly realized the reason he was not a Christian was due to his reluctance to forsake his sin. He confessed that from his early youth he had been praying, "Give me chastity and continency, only not yet." (*Confessions of St. Augustine*, Book VII, Paragraph 17).

The third step is to *believe God's promise* of forgiveness and cleansing. We must face ourselves with the reality of God's Word and what this verse (I John 1:9) means today in a very personal and practical way. In the light of our sin, we must come to a clear understanding of what divine forgiveness and cleansing will mean in our lives. And then we must believe God and fully take Him at His Word.

The fourth step is to *receive Jesus Christ* into our lives as the specific cleansing and enablement which our sin demands. Jesus Christ is not only our Savior, He is our sanctification and power (I Cor. 1:24, 30). He came and performed the work of salvation. This initial step in the Christian life is spoken of in the Bible as the blueprint for how we are to progress in daily life (Col. 2:6). Therefore, when we are in need of a specific cleansing and enablement, it is well to be exact in our decision of faith. If we need help in the area of gossip, it would be well to say, "Heavenly Father, having confessed to You my sin of being a gossip and having promised to forsake my sin entirely, I do now deliberately and in faith receive Jesus Christ into my life as my cleansing from gossip and as my enablement to live above this sin."

The fifth step is to *take God at His Word and live accordingly*. He has promised to forgive us and to cleanse us from our sin when we genuinely confess. Having confessed our sin as an act of faith, we must now rely on the faithfulness and justice of God. If we have confessed, we are forgiven and

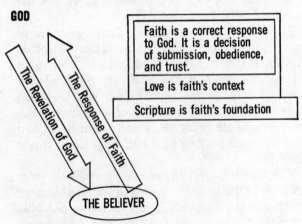

GOD

The Revelation of God

The Response of Faith

Faith is a correct response to God. It is a decision of submission, obedience, and trust.

Love is faith's context

Scripture is faith's foundation

THE BELIEVER

Diagram 15. *The key to success:* Accept the truth—faith is not a feeling but a decision! Deliberately choose to respond to God. Honestly surrender to God and His Word, sincerely face your need, and make the correct decision of obedience in complete trust.

we have been cleansed. When temptation comes, as it surely will, we must simply maintain our decision of faith, believing that the sin has already been dealt with, and refuse the temptation. As long as we continue this dependence on God and genuinely desire to be free from that sin, we will have the continuing grace and power of God to be free (John 8:32, 36). The promise of God is clear. He has said that if we respond to Him obediently in faith and love, He will come and work in us by His grace and power (Rom. 6:16-18; Phil. 2:12, 13; I Peter 1:22). (See Diagram 15.)

Questions for Discussion

1. Describe faith.

2. What did every person mentioned in Hebrews 11 manifest as part of his or her faith?

3. How important is the *amount* of faith we have?

4. Abraham is set forth in Scripture as an example of what?

5. According to Galatians 5:6, faith can be made to work in our lives only as a result of what?

6. What is the most serious hindrance to faith in the life of a Christian?

7. According to Romans 10:17, how do we get faith?

8. How does faith grow?

9. What did St. Augustine testify?

10. What do we experience when we confess our sin and failure as an act of faith?

Chapter 11

"And now faith demands . . ."

Faith demands   a correct beginning.

In the first chapter we stated that the Christian must first learn the truths of Christianity and then how to put them into practice. This last chapter is a statement on "practice." It will explain the most important element of "practice" which is a decision of faith. So there will be no misunderstanding, the necessary decisions of faith will be explained and suggested prayers will be given.

How does one approach the true and living God? The attitude that just any approach will do could hardly be more incorrect. God is infinite, eternal, and absolute holiness. We can come to God only in the way *He* has specified and ordained. Jesus Christ said, "I am the way, the truth, and the life: no man cometh unto the Father, but by me" (John 14:6).

The non-Christian may come to God only through Jesus Christ. A correct beginning means a sincere and thorough repentance for sin, a wholehearted surrender to the authority of Jesus Christ and His Word, and a deliberate, specific decision to receive Jesus Christ as Lord and Savior. The following prayer may help:

> Eternal God, I bow before You in a sincere and honest confession that I am a sinner and that I have sinned against You. I repent of my sin and apologize to You for all I have done. I completely surrender to Your authority and control as You have stated it in the Bible. On the basis of Your Word, Lord Jesus, I do now receive You into my life as my Lord and Savior. I believe in You and accept You as my forgiveness, cleansing, righteousness, and eternal life. I want to thank You for making all of this possible. In Jesus' name, Amen (Luke 13:3; Acts 17:30; John 1:12; 3:16-18, 36; 5:14; 8:24; Rom. 5:1; 8:1; 10:9, 10; I John 1:9; Rev. 3:20).

The Christian is in an entirely different relationship to God than the non-Christian. However, we may likewise come to God only through Jesus Christ. As believers, the issue in our lives is no longer that of initial salvation; we have been accepted and forgiven. The issue is now daily obedience.

How are we as Christians to approach God through Jesus Christ? We may come only in the way which is in harmony with the person of Jesus Christ, His work, and His Word. Who He is, what He has done in history, and what He has said in

127

His Word are the determining factors in our approach to God. A correct beginning, therefore, must be with complete sincerity and honesty. One may not pretend with God! All hypocrisy, sham, platitudes, pride, playing-the-game, and mask-wearing must be deliberately and honestly abandoned. We must decisively surrender *ourselves* to God. We must begin with ourselves, as we bow before God, and acknowledge that all failure in practice is our failure as a person. No elusive side-stepping of this basic truth may be tolerated.

However, we must do more than acknowledge our failures of faith and love. To meet the demand of faith, we must put the Word of God into practice. We must, therefore, personally assume the responsibility for being the right kind of person and for living in harmony with the person, work, and Word of God. No decision is greater nor more important than this. All other correct decisions find their roots here:

> Heavenly Father, I bow before You in a sincere and honest choice to surrender myself wholly to You as You have made Yourself known to me in Holy Scripture. I accept Your Word as my only authoritative standard for all of my life and activity. Therefore, I make the decision not to judge You, Your work, myself, nor others on the basis of my feelings or circumstances. (Rom. 12:1, 2; John 15:7, 10; Rom. 10:17; I Cor. 4:3-5; II Cor. 10:12).

Faith demands a correct attitude toward God.

To approach the true and living God correctly, we must come to Him in the attitude of worship and praise. God is worthy of all glory which could be given to Him. The highest deed which can be performed by man and the most essential is that of true worship. To come to God in selfishness, with our minds filled only with our own needs, is not the correct attitude. The reality of the true and living God, who is pure spirit, infinite, eternal and unchangeable in His being, wisdom, power, holiness, truth, and love, should compel us to worship Him with our total being. Any failure to do so indicates our ignorance of the greatness and goodness of the triune God.

The slightest reflection on the greatness of God, as manifested in His work as the Creator and Sustainer of all things, as the Governor of all nations, the Author of history, the Head of the church, the Lord of the harvest, and the Savior of mankind, should likewise cause us to bow before Him in adoration and praise.

Faith, therefore, demands that we recognize the greatness and goodness of God and worship Him for who He is and what He has done. It may be helpful to use the following affirmation.

I bow to acknowledge that You, the triune God, are worthy of all honor, praise, and worship as the Creator, Sustainer, and End of all things. As my Creator, I recognize that You made me for Yourself. I, therefore, choose to live for You. I am grateful that You loved me and chose me in Jesus Christ in eternity past and proved Your love by sending Your Son to die in my place. I praise You for every provision which has already been made for my past, present, and future needs through the representative work of Jesus Christ in whom

I have been quickened, raised, seated in the heavenlies, and anointed with the Holy Spirit (Rev. 4:11; Rom. 12:1, 2; 5:6-11; 8:28-39; Phil. 1:6; 4:6, 7, 13, 19; Eph. 1:3; 2:5, 6; Acts 2:1-4, 33).

Faith demands a correct understanding of the permanence of salvation.

Worshiping and honoring God are not acts performed only on our knees. They involve every part of our life and day. One of the most serious ways in which we dishonor God is to doubt His Word, either through ignorance or, worse yet, through presumptuous choice. A crucial area in this regard has to do with the possession of salvation. Our shallow understanding of the profound depths of divine redemption easily propels us into ingratitude and gnawing doubt. As a result, we judge God and evaluate His work and love on the basis of feeling and circumstance. This we may not do.

It is important to understand the provision God has made for us and to accept decisively as the truth what He has said in His Word concerning our salvation. The following prayer is an illustration of how this may be done:

Since I have received Your Son the Lord Jesus Christ as my Lord and Savior, I believe Your Word that You have received me, forgiven me, adopted me into Your family, assumed every responsibility for me, given to me eternal life, and made me complete in Christ. I accept the truth of Your Word that the Lord Jesus offers Himself

130

to me as my daily sufficiency through prayer and
the decisions of faith, and that the Holy Spirit
Himself has baptized me into the Body of Christ,
sealed me, anointed me for life and service, seeks
to lead me into a deeper walk with the Lord
Jesus and to fill my life with Himself. I accept
these truths as realities in my life today (John
1:12; Eph. 1:6, 7; John 17:11, 17, 21, 24; Eph.
1:5; Phil. 1:6; John 3:36; I John 5:9-13; Col. 2:10;
I Cor. 1:30; Col. 1:27; Gal. 2:20; John 14:13, 14;
Matt. 21:22; Rom. 6:1-19; Heb. 4:1-3, 11; I Cor.
12:13; Eph. 1:13, 14; Acts 1:8; John 7:37-39;
14:16-18; 15:26, 27; 16:13-15; Rom. 8:11-16; Eph.
5:18).

Faith demands a correct evaluation of sin and
holiness.

To honor and glorify God in daily life, faith demands that we understand and evaluate sin and
holiness correctly. The Christian has the awesome
ability to obey God and thereby bring holiness
into his life, or to disobey God and thereby bring
sin into his life. The kind of person we will become in character and practice is determined by
the choices we make today. Our future is an un-
developed potentiality for good and evil. Our
manner of life in the future is determined by the
sort of person we will be and this in turn is determined by our evaluation of sin and holiness
today. It is impossible to sin and escape the de-
structive force sin has on our character. Likewise,
obedience to God will bring strength and virtue
of character.

As Christians, therefore, we must take a stand against our own sinful nature and the temptations from without and within. We must choose to live according to the will of God and to be characterized by the holiness which is both the demand and the promise of God.

An important step in this direction is the acknowledgment of our inability to cope with sin and our inability to produce a holy character. The secret of sanctification is not found in our own resolutions or desires; it is found in Jesus Christ and His work within us, through the ministry of the Holy Spirit (Rom. 8:1-17; I Cor. 1:30).

I acknowledge in Your presence that only You can deal with my sin and only You can produce holiness in my life. In both of these areas I am dependent on You and Your grace. I, therefore, choose to wholly surrender myself to You to obey Your Word. I recognize that You have made every necessary provision for my daily life so that I may fulfil Your will and call. Therefore, I will not make excuses for my sin and failure. I renounce all self-effort to live the Christian life and to perform Christian service. I renounce all the sinful religious activity which only weeps over sin and failure. I renounce the sinful praying which would ask You to change circumstances and people so that I may be more spiritual. I renounce all drawing back from the work of the Holy Spirit within and the call of God without. And I renounce all those motives, goals, and activities which have served my sinful pride (I Cor. 1:30; II Cor. 9:8; Gal. 2:20; I John 5:4; Rom. 6:16-20; I Thess. 5:24).

Faith demands a correct response to the commands of God.

Faith is essentially a decision, made in dependence on God, in response to the promises and commands of the Scripture. When such decisions are made and put into practice, the grace of God flows into our lives, and we are increasingly set free from sin and enabled to live a holy life (Rom. 6:11-22; Phil. 2:12, 13; I Peter 1:22).

The secret of a successful Christian life is, therefore, rooted in the Word of God and in the believer's sincere response to God and His Word. There is no other place to begin. Everything in practical Christianity begins with God, His Word, and the individual's decision to respond correctly to God. When we know the biblical commandments regarding personal sanctification, honestly desire to obey God and make the right decisions of faith, then, and only then, will we know the will, grace, and power of God in our daily lives.

The demand of faith, therefore, is threefold. First, we must know the commands and promises of God. Second, we must possess a sincere and honest desire to obey and believe God. Third, we must acquire the knowledge of how to make a decision of faith and follow through by making such decisions.

In the New Testament there are four basic commands regarding the believer's daily life. All of the other commands and exhortations may be subsumed under these four or may be said to be their fulfillment.

133

These four commands are the application in the believer's daily life of the four historical deeds of redemption upon which all of Christianity rests. What the crucifixion, resurrection, ascension, and Pentecost imply and demand in our daily lives has been summarized into these four specific commands.

Because the Lord Jesus Christ was crucified as our representative so that we may be cleansed from the power of our inner law of sin, we have been commanded to "put off . . . the old man" (Eph. 4:22):

I now make the decision, Lord Jesus, to receive You as my sanctification, particularly now as my cleansing from sin, and ask You, blessed Holy Spirit, to apply to me the work of the crucifixion. Cleanse me from my pride, hypocrisy, lust, selfishness, doubt, and jealousy which I confess as sin. In cooperation with and dependence on You, I make the decision of faith to "put off the old man" (Rom. 6:1-22; I Cor. 1:30; Gal. 5:6-21; Eph. 4:22; Col. 3:1-17).

Because the Lord Jesus Christ was resurrected as our representative so that we may be enabled to live free from sin in holiness of life, we have been commanded to "put on the new man" (Eph. 4:24):

I now make the decision, Lord Jesus, to receive You as my sanctification, particularly now as my enablement, moment by moment to live above sin, and I do ask You, blessed Holy Spirit, to apply to me the work of the resurrection so

134

that I may walk in newness of life. I sincerely desire to have humility, honesty, purity, love, faith, and longsuffering in my daily life. In co-operation with and dependence on You, I make the decision of faith to "put on the new man" (Rom. 6:1-4; Gal. 5:22-26; Eph. 4:24).

Because the Lord Jesus Christ ascended as our representative to provide deliverance from Satan, we have been commanded to resist the devil (Eph. 4:27):

I now make the decision, Lord Jesus, to re-ceive You as my deliverance from Satan and by faith take my position with You in the heavenlies. I do ask You, blessed Holy Spirit, to apply to me the work of the ascension. I would wholly sur-render to You and, in the name of Jesus Christ, take my stand against all satanic influence and subtlety. In cooperation with the dependence on You, I make the decision of faith to resist the devil. (Eph. 1:17-23; 2:1-6; 4:27; 6:10-18; Col. 1:13; Heb. 2:14, 15; James 4:7; I Peter 5:8, 9).

Because the Lord Jesus Christ received the Holy Spirit as our representative and bestowed Him on His church, we have been commanded to "be filled with the Spirit" (Eph. 5:18):

I now make the decision to receive You, blessed Holy Spirit, as my anointing for every area of my life. I ask You, in all sincerity, to bring my character and life into full conformity to the person of Jesus Christ and the will of God. Please work with me so that Jesus Christ may be glori-fied and the fruit of Your presence may be seen

135

in my life. In cooperation with the dependence on You, I make the decision of faith to be "filled with the Spirit" (John 7:37-39; 14:16, 17, 26; 15:26, 27; 16:7-15; Acts 1:8; 2:33; Rom. 8:1-17; Eph. 5:18).

Faith demands a correct dependence on the faithfulness of God.

And now that we have responded to God and have obeyed His commands by making the necessary decisions of faith, what is the next step? It is simply to believe God and to live accordingly. When we are faced with a temptation or choice which would be contradictory to the person and deeds of God, the Word of God, and our decisions of faith, that form of thinking and acting must be rejected in dependence on God and as a reaffirmation of our faith. If we have sincerely made the decisions of faith and honestly desire to live accordingly, we can expect the wisdom, grace, and power to live a successful Christian life.

Having made this confession and these decisions of faith, I now take as my own Your promised rest for this day. I relax in the trust of faith knowing that in the moment of temptation, trial, or need, You will be there to be my strength and sufficiency. (Heb. 4:1-13; I Cor. 10:13).

For the sake of clarity and convenience, the prayers given above are here compiled with some amplification. The Bible references are presented so the various concepts may be found in the Scripture and utilized for further study. (See Diagram 16.)

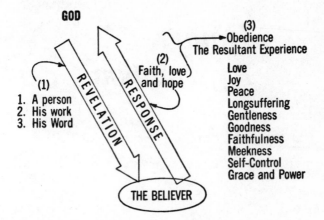

Diagram 16. *The key to success:* One must understand and practice three important truths:

1. *God as revealed Himself.* The content of God's revelation is primarily a person (Jesus Christ the living Word); the work of Jesus Christ in history (the crucifixion, resurrection, ascension, and Pentecost is how He has revealed Himself); and the Word of Jesus Christ (the inspired and infallible Scripture).

2. *The correct response to God's revelation is that of faith, love, and hope.* Faith and love are inseparable. Both must be present for either to work. The activity of faith and love (putting the Bible into practice by decisions of faith) is described in Scripture as "obedience." Hope accompanies faith and love.

3. *The resultant experience is the fruit of the Holy Spirit in grace and power.* While not denying that faith is an experience of grace and power it is encouraging to realize that, when we correctly respond to God in obedience, the automatic result will be an experience of grace and power through the ministry of the Holy Spirit. If the believer does not "enjoy the Lord" it is evident that he is in some way out of the will of God.

137

Daily Affirmation

Today I deliberately choose to submit myself fully to God as He has made Himself known to me through the Holy Scriptures which I honestly accept as the only inspired, infallible, authoritative standard for all of life and practice. In this day I will not judge God, His work, myself, or others on the basis of feelings or circumstances.

1. I recognize by faith that the triune God is worthy of all honor, praise, and worship as the Creator, Sustainer, and End of all things. I confess that God, as my Creator, made me for Himself. In this day I therefore choose to live for Him (Rev. 5:9, 10; Isa. 43:1, 7, 21; Rev. 4:11).
2. I recognize by faith that God loved me and chose me in Jesus Christ before time began (Eph. 1:1-7).

3. I recognize by faith that God has proven His love to me in sending His Son to die in my place; in Christ every provision has already been made for my past, present, and future needs through His representative work; and I have been quickened, raised, seated with Jesus Christ in the heavenlies, and anointed with the Holy Spirit (Rom. 5:6-11; 8:28-39; Phil. 1:6; 4:6, 7, 13, 19; Eph. 1:3; 2:5, 6; Acts 2:1-4, 33).

4. I recognize by faith that God has accepted me, since I have received Jesus Christ as my Lord and Savior (John 1:12; Eph. 1:6); that He has forgiven me (Eph. 1:7); adopted me into His family, assuming every responsibility for me (John 17:11, 12; Eph. 1:5; Phil. 1:6); given me eternal life (John 3:36; I John 5:9-13); applied the perfect righteousness of Christ to me so that I am now justified (Rom. 5:1; 8:3, 4; 10:4); made me complete in Christ (Col. 2:10); who offers Himself to me as my daily sufficiency through prayer and the decisions of faith (I Cor. 1:30; Col. 1:27; Gal. 2:20; John 14:13, 14; Matt. 21:22; Rom. 6:1-19; Heb. 4:1-3, 11).

5. I recognize by faith that the Holy Spirit has baptized me into the body of Christ (I Cor. 12:13); sealed me (Eph. 1:13, 14); anointed me for life and service (Acts 1:8; John 7:37-39); seeks to lead me into a deeper walk with Jesus Christ (John 14:16-18; 15:26, 27; 16:13-15; Rom. 8:11-16); and to fill my life with Himself (Eph. 5:18).

6. I recognize by faith that only God can deal with sin and only God can produce holiness of life. I confess that in my salvation my part

was only to receive Him and that He dealt with my sin and saved me. Now I confess that in order to live a holy life, I can only surrender to His will and receive Him as my sanctification; trusting Him to do whatever may be necessary in my life, without and within, so I may be enabled to live today in purity, freedom, rest, and power for His glory (John 1:12; I Cor. 1:30; II Cor. 9:8; Gal. 2:20; Heb. 4:9; I John 5:4; Jude 24).

Having confessed that God is worthy of all praise, that the Scriptures are the only authoritative standard, that only God can deal with sin and produce holiness of life, I again recognize my total dependence on Him and submission to Him. I accept the truth that praying in faith is absolutely necessary for the realization of the will and grace of God in my daily life (I John 5:14, 15; James 2:6; 4:2, 3; 5:16-18; Phil. 4:6, 7; Heb. 4:1-13; 11:6, 24-28).

Recognizing that faith is a total response to God by which the daily provisions the Lord has furnished in Himself are appropriated—I, therefore, make the following decisions of faith:

1. For this day (Heb. 3:7, 13, 15; 4:7) I make the decision of faith to surrender wholly to the authority of God as He has revealed Himself in the Scripture—to obey Him. I confess my sin, face the sinful reality of my old nature, and deliberately choose to walk in the light, in step with Christ, throughout the hours of this day (Rom. 6:16-20; Phil. 2:12; I John 1:7, 9).

140

2. For this day I make the decision of faith to surrender wholly to the authority of God as revealed in the Scripture—to believe Him. I accept only His Word as final authority. I now believe that since I have confessed my sin, He has forgiven and cleansed me (I John 1:9). I accept at full value His Word of promise, to be my sufficiency and rest, and will conduct myself accordingly (Exod. 33:14; I Cor. 1:30; II Cor. 9:8; Phil. 4:19).

3. For this day I make the decision of faith to recognize that God has made every provision so that I may fulfill His will and calling. Therefore, I will not make any excuse for my sin and failure (I Thess. 5:24).

4. For this day I make the decision of faith deliberately to receive from God that provision which He has made for me. I renounce all self-effort to live the Christian life and to perform God's service; renounce all sinful activity which only weeps over sin and failure; renounce all sinful praying which asks God to change circumstances and people so that I may be more spiritual; renounce all drawing back from the work of the Holy Spirit within and the call of God without; and renounce all non-biblical motives, goals and activities which serve my sinful pride.

   a. I now sincerely receive Jesus Christ as my sanctification, particularly as my cleansing from sin, and ask the Holy Spirit to apply to me the work Christ accomplished for me in the crucifixion. In co-operation with the dependence on Him, I obey the command to "put off the old man" (Rom. 6:1-14; I Cor. 1:30; Gal. 6:14; Eph. 4:22).

b. I now sincerely receive Jesus Christ as my sanctification, particularly as my enablement moment by moment to live above sin, and ask the Holy Spirit to apply to me the work of the resurrection so that I may walk in newness of life. I confess that only God can deal with my sin and only God can produce holiness and the fruit of the Spirit in my life. In cooperation with and dependence on Him, I obey the command to "put on the new man" (Rom. 6:1-14; Eph. 4:24).

c. I now sincerely receive Jesus Christ as my deliverance from Satan and take my position with Him in the heavenlies, asking the Holy Spirit to apply to me the work of the ascension. In His name I submit myself to God and stand against all satanic influence and subtlety. In cooperation with and dependence on God, I obey the command to resist the devil (Eph. 1:20-23; 2:5, 6; 4:27; 6:10-18; Col. 1:13; Heb. 2:14, 15; James 4:7; I Peter 3:22; 5:8, 9).

d. I now sincerely receive the Holy Spirit as my anointing for every aspect of life and service for today. I fully open my life to Him to fill me afresh in obedience to the command to "be filled with the Holy Spirit" (Eph. 5:18; John 7:37-39; 14:16, 17, 26; 15:26, 27; 16:7-15; Acts 1:8).

Having made this confession and these decisions of faith, I now receive God's promised rest for this day (Heb. 4:1-13). Therefore, I relax in the trust of faith, knowing that in the moment of temptation, trial, or need, the Lord Himself will be there as my strength and sufficiency (I Cor. 10:13).

Questions for Discussion

1. In John 14:6 the Lord Jesus declared that He is the way to God. To whom does this statement apply?

2. What is the most important decision a person can make once he has become a Christian?

3. What is the highest and noblest occupation in which a Christian can engage?

4. What should a person do if he doubts his salvation?

5. What should a Christian do when confronted with the problem of his sinful desires?

6. Where do we begin putting into practice the principles of holy living?

7. What four basic commands regarding the believer's daily life are found in the New Testament?

8. In your own words, sum up the principle and practice of living a victorious Christian life.

9. Why is it so important that we deliberately choose to submit ourselves fully to God?

10. Where in the Bible do we read that the Lord Himself will be the strength and sufficiency of those who trust Him even in the moment of temptation, trial, and need?

The Warfare Prayer

Heavenly Father, I bow in worship and praise before You. I cover myself with the blood of the Lord Jesus Christ as my protection. I surrender myself completely and unreservedly in every area of my life to You. I take a stand against all the workings of Satan that would hinder me in my prayer life. I address myself only to the true and living God and refuse any involvement of Satan in my prayer.

Satan, I command you, in the name of the Lord Jesus Christ, to leave my presence with all of your demons. I bring the blood of the Lord Jesus Christ between us.

Heavenly Father, I worship You and give You praise. I recognize that You are worthy to receive all glory and honor and praise. I renew my allegiance to You and pray that the blessed Holy Spirit will enable me in this time of prayer. I am thankful, heavenly Father, that You have loved me from past eternity and that You sent the Lord Jesus Christ into the world to die as my substitute. I am thankful that the Lord Jesus Christ came as my representative and that through Him You have completely forgiven me; You have adopted me into Your family; You have assumed all responsibility for me; You have given me eternal life; You have given me the perfect righteousness of the Lord Jesus Christ so I am now justified. I am thankful that in Him You have made me complete, and that You have offered Yourself to me to be my daily help and strength.

Heavenly Father, open my eyes that I may see how great You are and how complete is Your provision for this day. I am thankful that the victory the Lord Jesus Christ won for me on the cross and in His resurrection has been given to me and that I am seated with the Lord Jesus Christ in the heavenlies. I take my place with Him in the heavenlies and recognize by faith that all wicked spirits and Satan himself are under my feet. I declare, therefore, that Satan and his wicked spirits are subject to me in the name of the Lord Jesus Christ.

I am thankful for the armor You have provided. I put on the girdle of truth, the breastplate of righteousness, the sandals of peace and the helmet of salvation. I lift up the shield of faith against all the fiery darts of the enemy; and I take into my hand the sword of the Spirit, the Word of God. I choose to use Your Word against all the forces of evil in my life. I put on this armor and live and pray in complete dependence upon You, blessed Holy Spirit.

I am grateful, heavenly Father, that the Lord Jesus Christ spoiled all principalities and powers and made a show of them openly and triumphed over them in Himself. I claim all victory for my life today. I reject all the insinuations, accusations, and temptations of Satan. I affirm that the Word of God is true and I choose to live today in the light of God's Word. I choose, heavenly Father, to live in obedience to You and in fellowship with You. Open my eyes and show me the areas of my life that do not please You. Work in me to cleanse me from all ground that would give Satan a foothold against me. I do in every way stand in all that it means to be Your adopted child and I welcome the ministry of the Holy Spirit.

By faith and in dependence on You I put off the old man and stand in all victory of the crucifixion where the Lord Jesus Christ provided cleansing from sin. I put on the new man and stand in all the victory of the resurrection and the provision He has made for me to live above sin.

Therefore, today I put off the old patterns of sin and selfishness and I put on the new nature with its love. I put off the old patterns of sin and fear and I put on the new nature with its courage. I put off the old patterns of sin with all its deceitful lusts and I put on the new nature with its righteousness, purity, and honesty.

In every way I stand in the victory of the ascension and glorification of the Lord Jesus Christ, whereby all the principalities and powers were made subject to Him. I claim my place in Christ as victorious with Him over all the enemies of my soul. Blessed Holy Spirit, I pray that You would fill me. Come into my life, break down every idol and cast out every foe.

I am thankful, heavenly Father, for the expression of Your will for my daily life as You have shown me in Your Word. I therefore claim all the will of God for today. I am thankful that You have blessed me with all spiritual blessings in heavenly places in Christ Jesus. I am thankful that You have begotten me unto a living hope by the resurrection of Jesus Christ from the dead. I am thankful that You have made a provision so that today I can live filled with the Spirit of God, with love and joy and peace, with longsuffering, gentleness, and goodness, with meekness, faithfulness, and self-control in my life. I recognize that this is Your will for me and I therefore reject and resist all the endeavors of Satan and his wicked spirits to rob me of the will of God. I refuse in this day to believe my feelings and I hold up the shield of faith against all the accusations and distortion and insinuations that Satan would put into my mind. I claim the fullness of the will of God for my life today.

In the name of the Lord Jesus Christ I completely surrender myself to You, heavenly Father, as a living sacrifice. I choose not to be conformed to this world. I choose to be transformed by the renewing of my mind, and I pray that You will show me Your will and enable me to walk in all fullness of Your will today.

I am thankful, heavenly Father, that the weapons of our warfare are not carnal but mighty through God to the pulling down of strongholds, to the casting down of imaginations and every high thing that exalteth itself against the knowledge of God, and to bring every thought into obedience to the Lord Jesus Christ. Therefore, in my own life today I tear down the strongholds of Satan and smash the plans of Satan that have been formed against me. I tear down the strongholds of Satan against my mind, and I surrender my mind to You, blessed Holy Spirit. I affirm, heavenly Father, that You have not given me the spirit of fear but of power, love, and a sound mind. I break and smash the strongholds of Satan formed against my emotions today. I give my will to You, and choose to make the right decisions of faith. I smash the strongholds of Satan formed against my body today. I give my body to You recognizing that I am Your temple. I rejoice in Your mercy and goodness.

Heavenly Father, I pray that now and through this day You will strengthen and enlighten me, show me the way Satan is hindering and tempting and lying and distorting the truth in my life. Enable me to be the kind of person that will please You. Enable me to be aggressive in prayer and faith. Enable me to be aggressive mentally, to think about and practice Your Word, and to give You Your rightful place in my life.

Again I cover myself with the blood of the Lord Jesus Christ and pray that You, Blessed Holy Spirit, will bring all the work of the crucifixion, the resurrection, the ascension, and Pentecost into my life today. I surrender myself to you. I refuse to be discouraged. You are the God of all hope. You have proven Your power by resurrecting Jesus Christ from the dead, and I claim in every way this victory over all satanic forces in my life. I pray in the name of the Lord Jesus Christ with thanksgiving. Amen.